The Cambridge Introduction to
Michel Foucault

The French philosopher and historian Michel Foucault is essential reading for students in departments of literature, history, sociology and cultural studies. His work on the institutions of mental health and medicine, the history of systems of knowledge, literature and literary theory, criminality and the prison system, and sexuality has had a profound and enduring impact across the humanities and social sciences. This introductory book, written for students, offers in-depth critical and contextual perspectives on all of Foucault's major published works. It provides ways in to understanding Foucault's key concepts of subjectivity, discourse and power, and explains the problems of translation encountered in reading Foucault in English. The book also explores the critical reception of Foucault's works and acquaints the reader with the afterlives of some of his theories, particularly his influence on feminist and queer studies. This book offers the ideal introduction to a famously complex, controversial and important thinker.

Lisa Downing is Professor of French Discourses of Sexuality and Director of the Centre for the Interdisciplinary Study of Sexuality and Gender in Europe at the University of Exeter.

The Cambridge Introduction to
Michel Foucault

LISA DOWNING

CAMBRIDGE
UNIVERSITY PRESS

CAMBRIDGE UNIVERSITY PRESS
Cambridge, New York, Melbourne, Madrid, Cape Town,
Singapore, São Paulo, Delhi, Tokyo, Mexico City

Cambridge University Press
The Edinburgh Building, Cambridge CB2 8RU, UK

Published in the United States of America by
Cambridge University Press, New York

www.cambridge.org
Information on this title: www.cambridge.org/9780521682992

First published 2008
Third printing 2010

A catalogue record for this publication is available from the British Library

Library of Congress Cataloguing in Publication Data

Downing, Lisa.
   The Cambridge introduction to Michel Foucault / Lisa Downing.
      p. cm.
   Includes bibliographical references and index.
   ISBN 978-0-521-86443-5 (hardback)
   1. Foucault, Michel, 1926–1984. I. Title.
   B2430.F724D69 2008
   194 – dc22   2008020089

ISBN 978-0-521-86443-5 Hardback
ISBN 978-0-521-68299-2 Paperback

Contents

Preface

> If you knew when you began a book what you would say at the end, do you
> think that you would have the courage to write it? The game is worthwhile
> in so far as we don't know what will be the end.
>
> Michel Foucault

A reading of the works of Michel Foucault (1926–84) does not so much equip
us with new pieces of knowledge, or even teach us new and different ways
of knowing. Rather, it invites us to share in a radical calling into question of
the ways in which knowledge itself operates. Foucault argues that all forms of
knowledge are historically relative and contingent, and cannot be dissociated
from the workings of power. Destabilising many of the key facets of Western
epistemology, he effectively lays bare their functioning. This agenda of demys-
tification, central to all of Foucault's work, encourages an uncommon way of
perceiving language, social structures and medical institutions, university disciplines, and sexual acts and identities. We are provided not with an alternative
theory of these domains, but with an awareness of the force fields of influence
that bring them into being and determine their meaning and operation in
given cultural and historical contexts. So different is this way of apprehending
knowledge that the reader new to Foucault, and to post-structuralist continen-
tal thought in general, may struggle with the rigorous challenges posed by his
guiding methodologies of 'archaeology' and 'genealogy'. This introduction to
the work of Michel Foucault, which situates his investigations in their intellectual and historical contexts, and which proceeds by a detailed discussion of
Foucault's major works available in English translation – both his full-length
books and numerous articles and interviews – is thus indispensable for any
student or other interested reader approaching his work for the first time.

It is helpful to think of Foucault's revisionist histories (archaeolo-
gies/genealogies) not as proposing entirely different versions of historical truth,
but as relativising correctives, as texts which teach us that if we only look at the
accepted and well-worn interpretations, we only appreciate a partial view of

history. So, in what is probably Foucault's best-known work, the first volume of *The History of Sexuality, The Will to Knowledge* (1976),[1] Foucault's critique of the 'repressive hypothesis' is not really intended to suggest that there were no censorious or prudish attitudes towards sex in Victorian Britain, because this would be the replacement of one totalising narrative with another. Rather, it sets out to show that this is *only half the picture*. It is by thinking *also* about that historical moment's obsession with inciting sexual confession, with naming types of sexual deviance and with producing what Foucault terms a proliferation of discourses about sex, that we see the fuller picture. At the broader level, it is also by engaging in this kind of game with history – for Foucault is nothing if not a magnificent game player – that we are afforded an insight into how Foucault thinks history works. The history of any cultural phenomenon always involves, alongside the commonsensical or authorised version of events, ulterior narratives, an unspoken set of truths, that often efface themselves as visible processes precisely as an effect of their operation within the larger grid of competing knowledge; authorised and unauthorised; normalising and dissident. One of Foucault's most striking and far-reaching points regarding power and knowledge is the insight that power operates according to and by means of secrecy and silence as well as – or instead of – by voicing its presence in loud and oppressive interdictions and orders.

The influence of Michel Foucault – a very French thinker – on the Anglo-American academic and reading public has grown in recent years, thanks to the incorporation of his corpus into the university curricula of contemporary literary studies, sexuality and gender studies, politics, and sociology. Accordingly, numerous introductory guides to Foucault, aimed at students and scholars in these various disciplines, have appeared from major academic presses. Despite their many and varied strengths, few of these works are primarily concerned with offering an accessible way in to reading Foucault for the student of literary and cultural studies. This, then, is the precise gap that *The Cambridge Introduction to Michel Foucault* will fill. It will offer an accessible but thorough introduction to the main works in Foucault's corpus and will assist readers in understanding their relevance for the analysis of the conditions of literary and cultural production and philosophical ideas.

In addition, the book will provide some other unique features. First, it will identify and address the problem faced by the English-speaking reader of having

---

[1] When referring to Foucault's works, I shall use the accepted English translated titles (or, for page references, the abbreviations of the same listed under 'Abbreviations', p. xi), but the dates, unless otherwise stated, will refer to the original year of publication of the first French edition.

to read Foucault in a not-always-accurate translation. A tendency of much Anglo-American criticism and the other critical introductions to Foucault is to write about the translations as if they were the original texts. I will avoid this reductive tendency, bringing attention where necessary to the features of the French texts that have been elided or flattened out in the translation process, distorting the meaning and resonance of Foucault's words; and I shall comment on receptions of the translations of Foucault's works and the misinterpretations that have arisen from these in existing Foucault criticism. Secondly, this book will address and explain the status of the French intellectual and the part played by this figure in French cultural and political life. Any introduction to a French thinker requires a very careful contextualisation of a specific intellectual 'scene'. Thirdly, it will engage in detail with Foucault's reflections on literature, including a chapter on his writings on the works of Bataille, Blanchot, Klossowski and Roussel, and his significant essay on the 'author function' ('What is an Author?', 1969), a work which is often omitted or treated in parentheses or footnotes in other introductory guides. I will argue that many of Foucault's key concerns and concepts – the critique of reason, anti-humanistic thinking, the problematisation of the subject – are best articulated when he takes literature as the object of his investigation. Finally, where relevant, this book will also briefly treat the rhetorical qualities of Foucault's own writing: qualities that have made his work unpopular with philosophers of the analytic tradition but endeared him to literary scholars. Following the example of Dan Beer's recent innovative monograph *Michel Foucault: Form and Power*,[2] *The Cambridge Introduction to Michel Foucault* will pay attention to what is important in Foucault's language and the ways in which his form enacts his meaning.

A further central concern of the analyses in this book will be to explore and chart Foucault's often apparently contradictory ideas about selfhood and subjectivity. A paradoxical suspicion of, and fascination with, the subject of experience runs through Foucault's corpus, resonating differently in the various texts, and causing some commentators on Foucault's life's work to accuse him of inconsistency and contradiction. From asserting the radical negation of the human being as the transcendental subject of knowledge and experience in *The Archaeology of Knowledge* (1969), Foucault moves on to a quest to theorise a controversial 'ethics of the self' in his final works, a project he was sketching at the time of his death in 1984, due to an 'AIDS-related' illness. The reason for placing 'AIDS-related' between scare quotes will become clear towards the close

---

[2] Dan Beer, *Michel Foucault: Form and Power* (Oxford: Legenda, European Humanities Research Association, 2002).

of the book, where I shall explore the legacy of Foucault's critiques of sexual knowledge and medical categories for late-twentieth-century sexuality studies.

The book comprises an introductory contextualising chapter followed by five further chapters, broadly structured along both chronological and thematic lines, each devoted to one or more of Foucault's major works; and concludes with a seventh and final chapter which charts some of the afterlives of Foucault's thinking. Chapter 1 takes the form of an introduction to the major intellectual and historical trends that influenced Foucault's thinking and determined the different methods and concerns of his works over the course of the twenty years during which he published. The next five chapters treat, in the following order, the institutions of psychiatry and medicine; the epistemology of the human sciences; literature and literary theory; criminality and punishment; sexuality, knowledge and power. The closing chapter treats the major reception of Foucault's work within the arts and humanities in the fields of feminism, gender and sexuality studies, and 'queer' theory. The book closes with a bibliography of selected titles designed to guide the reader's further study and point him or her towards specialised works on the different aspects, receptions and intertexts of Foucault's work.

I would like to acknowledge the help of Peter Cryle, Tim Dean, Robert Gillett, Dany Nobus and Elizabeth Stephens, who were stimulating and generous interlocutors about Foucault during my preparation of this book, and some of whom lent me materials to which I would otherwise not have had access. I would also like to thank Simon Gaunt, who invited me to present a paper on Foucault in a panel on 'Queer Theory in France' at the Society for French Studies' annual conference in July 2007, where I was able to discuss a version of the final chapter of this book with the learned audience and my fellow panel members, Hector Kollias and Jason Hartford. Finally, thanks are due to Ray Ryan at Cambridge University Press for being a most patient Commissioning Editor.

Abbreviations

Published collections of Foucault's lectures, essays, seminars and interviews referred to in the book

A   *Abnormal: Lectures at the Collège de France, 1974–1975*, ed. Valerio Marchetti and Antonella Salomoni, trans. Graham Burchell (London and New York: Verso, 2003)

DE   *Dits et écrits 1954–1988*, ed. Daniel Defert and François Ewald, four volumes (Paris: Gallimard, 1994)

EW i   *The Essential Works of Michel Foucault 1954–1988*, vol. 1, *Ethics: Subjectivity and Truth*, ed. Paul Rabinow, trans. Robert Hurley *et al.* (New York: New York Press, 1997)

EW ii   *The Essential Works of Michel Foucault 1954–1988*, vol. 2, *Aesthetics: Method and Epistemology*, ed. James Faubion, trans. Robert Hurley *et al.* (New York: New York Press, 1998)

EW iii *The Essential Works of Michel Foucault 1954–1988*, vol. 3, *Power*, ed. James Faubion, trans. Robert Hurley *et al.* (New York: New York Press, 2000)

FL   *Foucault Live: Interviews 1966–84*, ed. Sylvère Lotringer (New York: Semiotext(e), 1989)

SMD   *Society Must be Defended: Lectures at the Collège de France, 1975–1976* (Harmondsworth: Penguin, 2004)

TS   *Technologies of the Self: A Seminar with Michel Foucault*, ed. Luther H. Martin, Huck Gutman and Patrick H. Hutton (Amherst: The University of Massachusetts Press, 1988)

Foucault's books

(The original French titles and dates of publication are given after the English
translations in square brackets.)

AK   *The Archaeology of Knowledge,* trans. A. M. Sheridan Smith (London
and New York: Routledge, 2002) [*L'Archéologie du savoir,* 1969]

BC   *The Birth of the Clinic: An Archaeology of Medical Perception,* trans.
A. M. Sheridan (London and New York: Routledge, 2003) [*Naissance de
la clinique,* 1963]

CS   *The Care of the Self, The History of Sexuality 3,* trans. Robert Hurley
(Harmondsworth: Penguin, 1990) [*Histoire de la sexualité 3: Le Souci de
soi,* 1984]

DL   *Death and the Labyrinth: The World of Raymond Roussel,* trans. Charles
Ruas, intro. John Ashbery (New York: Doubleday and Co., 1986)
[*Raymond Roussel,* 1963]

DP   *Discipline and Punish,* trans. Alan Sheridan (Harmondsworth: Penguin,
1991) [*Surveiller et punir,* 1975]

HB   *Herculine Barbin; Being the Recently Discovered Memoirs of a Nineteenth-
Century French Hermaphrodite,* trans. Richard McDougall (Brighton:
Harvester Press, 1990) [*Herculine Barbin dite Alexandre B,* 1978]

HM   *History of Madness,* ed. Jean Khalfa, trans. Jonathan Murphy and Jean
Khalfa (London and New York: Routledge, 2006) [*Folie et déraison:
Histoire de la folie à l'âge classique,* 1961]

IPR *I, Pierre Rivière, Having Slaughtered My Mother, My Sister and My
Brother: A Case of Parricide in the Nineteenth Century,* trans. Frank
Jellinek (Lincoln and London: University of Nebraska Press, 1975)
[*Moi, Pierre Rivière, ayant égorgé ma mère, ma sœur et mon frère: un cas
de parricide au dix-neuvième siècle,* 1973]

MC   *Madness and Civilization: A History of Insanity in the Age of Reason,*
trans. Richard Howard (London and New York: Routledge, 2001)
[based on an abridged edition of *Folie et déraison: Histoire de la folie à
l'âge classique,* 1961]

OT   *The Order of Things,* trans. Alan Sheridan (London and New York:
Routledge, 1989) [*Les Mots et les choses,* 1966]

UP   *The Use of Pleasure, The History of Sexuality 2,* trans. Robert Hurley
(Harmondsworth: Penguin, 1992) [*Histoire de la sexualité 2: L'Usage des
plaisirs,* 1984]

WK   *The Will to Knowledge, The History of Sexuality 1,* trans. Robert Hurley
(Harmondsworth: Penguin, 1990) [*Histoire de la sexualité 1: La Volonté
de savoir,* 1976]

Chapter 1

Life, texts, contexts

I don't find it necessary to know exactly what I am. The main interest in life and work is to become someone else that you were not in the beginning.

Michel Foucault

Didier Eribon opens his biography of Foucault with the following assertion: 'Writing a biography of Michel Foucault may seem paradoxical. Did he not on numerous occasions, challenge the notion of the author, thereby dismissing the very possibility of biographical study?'[1] Having presented this problem, Eribon procedes with the caveat: 'even so, Foucault could not isolate himself from the society in which he lived. He, like everyone else, was forced to fulfil the "functions he described".'[2] Throughout this book, and particularly in this opening chapter on Foucault's intellectual and social contexts, I will be sensitive to the particular tension raised by the prospect of writing about the life and influences of Michel Foucault, a thinker who insisted many times that the self should be an ongoing process of creation rather than a fixed identity or personality. As he famously remarked: 'Do not ask me who I am and do not ask me to remain the same' (*AK*, p. 19). Instead of trying to make him remain the same, then, instead of uniting the various Foucaldian voices, I shall provide an introduction to his texts, and to the contexts from which they arise, that is broadly sympathetic to his critique of biographical criticism.

In this chapter, I will discuss the complex interplay of ideas, political events and currents of thought that influenced the period in which he was writing and shaped the kinds of texts and ideas that bear the author name 'Foucault'.[3] Here and in later chapters I will also address the various perceptions of Michel Foucault as a public, political figure, and the difficulty of reconciling Foucault's

1

actions with some of his ideas. Most prominent among these is the disjuncture – which may also be read as a productive tension – between his involvement in direct prisoners' activism in the 1970s and the genealogical theorisation of the prison system in *Discipline and Punish* (1975), which does not straightforwardly seek a reformatory or liberationist agenda with regard to conditions in prisons, but instead shows that techniques developed in a carceral context extend everywhere into modern life. The book thus constitutes a critique of a society that has internalised an idea of carceral power, but not a call to arms against the workings of a particular institution.

Foucault's oft-commented-on suspicion of the notion that the self is a transparent entity that can be accurately or usefully written about, or wholly divulged to – or by – the other, is in sympathy with the ideas of other prominent thinkers of his epoch and place. These include Louis Althusser, who attempted to remove any traces of humanism from Marxist theory, and Jacques Lacan, whose poststructuralist psychoanalysis restored the most anarchic aspects of the Freudian text in a direct refusal of the primacy of the ego so central to American psychology at the time. Foucault's problematisation of the social self is a largely political project, at least in later works. In *Discipline and Punish* and *The Will to Knowledge*, it is made clear that the modern self is constituted through, and by means of, the operations of various kinds of disciplinary mechanisms acting on the body. Accepting the notion of an independent or transparent self would be a dangerous undertaking, even if it were possible, as it would ignore the operations of these systems of knowledge, and our internalisation of them. Ultimately, Foucault's work reveals how we are both *subject to* and *the subjects of* the workings of power relations. This is an idea he expresses via the concept of *assujettissement*, a term carrying different valencies of meaning at different moments in the corpus of works, valencies often flattened out by the translation process.

The Foucaldian notions of 'self' and 'subject', then, are paradoxical ones. They describe at once, and intriguingly, a historical and political agent (affecting history by accessing the impersonal and productive workings of power and resistance) and the *effect of* the operations of historical processes. Foucault is initially dubious of the 'cult of the self', since that self would simply be a set of internalised social norms and expectations, and yet he becomes fascinated in his final works with our individual potential to exploit the constructed nature of the self as a project. In his theoretical exploratory works on the 'care of the self' and the ethics and aesthetics of pleasure (volumes two and three of *The History of Sexuality*), and in interviews given in the USA shortly before his death, he plays with the question of how one might – in Nietzsche's words – '"give style" to one's character – a great and rare art'.[4] It is this concern with the self – an individual self understood at times as the effects of discourse and yet at others as the agent of resistance and transgression; a radical ethical and aesthetic subject effecting self-stylisation – that is one of the most intriguing features of Foucault's later texts. The playfulness of Foucault's project – the way in which he tends to parody the discourses he is critiquing and to take oppositional positions at certain moments for strategic reasons, even if he later makes productive use of the very propositions he was earlier critiquing; and the chameleon-like nature of his ideas about the agency of the self discussed above – all make Foucault a challenging, difficult, but always entertaining writer.

Intellectual contexts

It is against the backdrop of a very particular intellectual climate that Michel Foucault's work must initially be understood. In post-Second-World-War France, existentialist phenomenology and Marxist thought provided the dominant and – to some extent – conflicting forces in intellectual life. The former, championed by the vibrant public intellectuals Jean-Paul Sartre and Simone de Beauvoir, attributed political agency and free will to individual consciousness, arguing that authentic freedom was a genuine possibility and that its assumption was a matter of responsibility for each citizen. In this regard, existentialism diverged from Marxism, as the latter dismissed the idea of individual free will as nothing more than a comforting bourgeois fiction, and held that only through collective struggle could the oppressed classes liberate themselves from the dominant classes. On some questions, however, existentialist phenomenology and Marxism converged. Sartre had a certain amount of respect for the French Communist Party owing to its strong Resistance activities during the occupation of France, though he never became a member of the Party himself, and he also admitted to the intellectual importance of Marxist thought. Sartre's commitment to political action – the French post-war ideal of *engagement* – made the intellectual into a prominent political figure rather than a reclusive scholar. Foucault was intellectually weaned on these debates and divisions, like all those of his generation, and the work he would go on to develop bears the traces of their influence, even if it is often expressed in the form of critique or resistance. Refusing to accept entirely any given or established position is very much a characteristic of Foucaldian rhetoric, resulting sometimes in apparent internal contradictions.

Foucault's relationship to existentialism is perhaps simpler to summarise than his position with regard to Marxist thought. Despite an early interest in the phenomenological works of Heidegger and Husserl, and his strategic use of the ideas of 'Daseinanalysis' (more on this later), the bulk of Foucault's work forms part of an explicit and politicised reaction against the 'philosophy of consciousness', associated primarily with Sartre, who throughout the 1950s and 1960s was the major intellectual figure in France. The French cultivation of philosophy as part of everyday life – as evidenced by its ubiquitous place on school and university curricula – means that an intellectual can occupy a very public national role in France, in a way that is more or less unheard of in the UK or USA. Sartre's embodiment of this role approximated something close to celebrity, a concept that Foucault despised. Like Sartre, however, Foucault himself would become something of a public intellectual, engaging openly with political struggles (May 1968, prisoners' rights) and combining commentary with direct activism. However, Foucault styled himself as a very different kind of intellectual to Sartre. He may have had Sartre's public persona partially in mind when he wrote of the 'teachers' who become 'public men with the same obligations' (*TS*, p. 9). Foucault thought that the intellectual should be not a 'universal' but a 'specific' intellectual. By 'universal intellectual', Foucault meant an academic posing as a 'master of truth and justice' and conveying general profundities to the masses (*EW iii*, p. 129). By contrast, the 'specific intellectual' would be a professional with direct access to, and specialist understanding of, a given scientific discipline or institution, and would be politically sensitised to the ways in which its local configurations of power present privileged forms of knowledge as if they are truths.[5] There is a 'grass roots' element to Foucault's thinking, then, which suggests his affinities with left-wing ideals and anti-bourgeois values. Uncovering and explaining the operation of the hidden workings of power is the principal task of the Foucaldian intellectual, even though Foucault himself did not identify wholly with any one 'specific' field, but rather commented on several, from plural perspectives.

To understand Foucault's relationship to Marxism, the reader must firstly be aware that intellectual Marxism and communist politics diverged considerably in the France of the 1950s and 1960s. Where intellectual Marxism had a reputation for being radical and progressive because it refused the 'philosophies of consciousness' that it dismissed as bourgeois, the French Communist Party (PCF) appeared to many to be excessively institutional and *doctrinaire*. Foucault was a member of the PCF only briefly.[6] Its failure to criticise the Soviet invasion of Hungary in 1956, as well as its anti-Semitic and homophobic politics, were particularly rebarbative to Foucault. Homophobia was a strong characteristic of mainstream interwar and post-war French culture, one which was particularly strongly pursued by the Vichy regime. In 1942, Amendment 334 was added to the Penal Code which raised the age of consent to twenty-one and made sex with a minor an offence punishable by a prison term of between six months and three years. 'Minors' indulging in consensual sex could also be prosecuted for assault. While the PCF would not have supported Vichy law, neither did it repudiate homophobia, a fact which must have seemed particularly harsh to a radical young homosexual entering the Communist Party. As Foucault has put it: 'I was never really integrated into the Communist Party because I was homosexual, and it was an institution that reinforced all the values of the most traditional bourgeois life.'[7] It is important, however, to dissociate Foucault's strong opposition to party dogma (and, indeed, to dogmatic politics in general – Foucault shied away from any long-term political allegiance, professing himself suspicious of the way in which political parties tend to organise themselves around charismatic leaders) from his continued intellectual interest in Marxist thought. Foucault would engage with Marx's analyses of power relations throughout the whole of his body of work, but his methodology diverged from that of Marx in a number of ways. Where Marx proposes a global philosophy, Foucault is concerned with specificity. Where Marx puts forward a system, Foucault seeks to demystify the working of systematisation. And – most significantly – where Marx locates power in the oppression of one group, the proletariat, who, via the raising of class consciousness, should be encouraged to throw off their shackles and aim for revolution, Foucault develops a model of power relations, a network or force field of influences which is never the unique preserve of the dominator over the dominated. One can argue that, as Foucault's work developed, it dissociated itself progressively from the Marxist agenda. It is only in his first book, *Maladie mentale et personnalité* (1954), that Foucault sets out an explicitly Marxist approach to his subject matter (here the institutionalisation of mental illness), an agenda which he later erased from subsequent editions of the work (starting with the first reprint in 1962). However, in *Discipline and Punish*, as late as 1975, the description of the coming into being of the *homo docilis* can be plausibly read as an alternative to Marx's description of the creation of a class of workers, and indeed Foucault refers directly in that text to the workings of 'state apparatuses', a term coined by his teacher and friend at the Ecole Normale Supérieure, the Marxist thinker Althusser. However, Foucault's position in *Discipline and Punish* ultimately differs from a Marxist analysis of class oppression, owing to the specific nature of the Foucaldian concept of *homo docilis* or disciplined body, which is found everywhere in society, not just in the toiling classes but in the classroom, the army and the prison, since the workings of what Foucault would call disciplinary power saturate the whole of society. I shall explore these ideas in more detail in Chapter 5.

Foucault's revised uses and interpretations of Marxist theory, and his disagreements with it, were in no small part indebted to his intellectual affiliations with Althusser, who was the leading intellectual of the French Communist Party. Both Althusser's and Foucault's works downplay the tendency to assert the primacy of human intentionality – in analysing the workings of the class system in Althusser's case, and in remapping the history of institutions in Foucault's. Althusser's reformulation of Marxist theory, which denudes it of its links with Stalinism as well as of any traces of humanism and subjectivity, bears certain similarities to Foucault's development of a theory of discourse as constitutive, rather than revelatory, of subjectivity.

The influence of other mentors, teachers and friends on the formation of Foucault's methodological and theoretical leanings must also be explored. Two of the most important of these are Georges Canguilhem and Georges Dumézil. Canguilhem's contribution to the philosophy of science, drawing on the works of Gaston Bachelard, was undoubtedly influential in shaping Foucault's early interest in, and approach to, the history of mental illness. Canguilhem denies the priority of the acting subject, focusing instead on the formation of knowledge and the concept. Foucault's suspicion of transparent models of subjectivity and his privileging of discontinuity over linear progress suggest the importance of Bachelard, via Canguilhem, to his method. Indeed, in explicitly aligning himself with the 'philosophy of concept' as opposed to the popular philosophies of consciousness or experience, Foucault was acknowledging this debt.

Georges Dumézil elaborated a reading method based on the awareness of a system of 'functional correlations between discursive formations', similar to the archaeological exploration of forms of knowledge essayed in Foucault's *The Order of Things* (1966) and *The Archaeology of Knowledge* (1969). Dumézil's method of discourse analysis was explicitly referenced in Foucault's inaugural address at the Collège de France in 1970 (published as *L'Ordre du discours* ['The Order of Discourse'], 1971) as a foundational influence on his work: 'it is he who taught me to analyse the internal economy of a discourse in a fashion completely different from the methods of traditional exegesis'.[8] Although the work of Dumézil is almost unknown in the Anglo-American world, he is significant as the proponent of a French structuralism of myth, long before the heyday of high structuralism.

Foucault's direction as a thinker, then, was driven by a desire to seek intellectual alternatives to – or, at least, critical variations on – the dominant poles of existentialism and Marxism and their philosophical debt to Hegelian dialectical historical thinking. The work of various contemporary thinkers, in a range of fields, provided models for thinking outside of the box. Some of these influences seem unlikely ones for Foucault, seen in the light of his corpus as a whole, but they provided specific insights for a given problem or project. When preparing his early work on mental illness, for example, Foucault was drawn to the therapeutic discourse of Daseinanalysis developed by Ludwig Binswanger and

Roland Kuhn. This therapy draws on Heideggerian phenomenological theories of experience, or 'being in the world', to explore psychical phenomena. (So, that which occurs for a Freudian psychoanalyst at the level of phantasy or dream occurs for the Daseinanalyst at the level of experience.) Works by Foucault on mental illness, sexual psychopathology and the 'dangerous individual' are also clearly influenced by Daseinanalysis' rejection of the therapeutic tendency to reduce individual suffering to the generic label or category. This is particularly clear in Foucault's critique of the psychiatric system's classification of the mentally ill, and sexology's construction of the modern sexual subject via a taxonomy of the perversions. However, Foucault's attitude to the notion of experience, central to a Heideggerian phenomenological perspective, mutates considerably at different points in his corpus. While declaring himself an exponent of Canguilhem's 'philosophy of the concept' rather than the 'philosophy of experience' prized by phenomenology, Foucault's critical interest in experience never the less persisted. His controversial *History of Madness* (1961) sought to inscribe a history of the experience of the mad, whose voice had been silenced by the authorised discourse of psychiatry and resurfaced only in fragments of writing. And in an essay on Canguilhem, Foucault tried to elaborate an account of experience as biological, as an alternative to the phenomenological notion of 'lived experience'.[9] Given Foucault's suspicion of the claims of biology elsewhere, we are reminded again of his tendency to use strategically whichever discourses and methodologies will allow him at any point to counter, or better *relativise*, a given target, even though those very discourses and methodologies may, at other times, themselves become the targets of demystifying work. At the beginning of *The Archaeology of Knowledge*, Foucault draws attention to a problem regarding his own conceptualisation of experience in his earlier work, *The History of Madness*, which 'accorded far too great a place, and a very enigmatic one too, to "experience", thus showing to what extent one was still close to admitting an anonymous and general subject of history' (*AK*, p. 18).[10] The anti-humanist archaeological project provided one way of denuding history of a general subject of experience. Later, Foucault would return more critically to a treatment of the question of experience in *The Will to Knowledge* and *The Use of Pleasure* (1984), where he argues that the subject's perception of him or herself in the light of an internalised discourse of 'truth' about his or her desire is fundamental to the functioning of modern sexual subjectivity.

Archaeology and structuralism

We are beginning to see how difficult it is to ascribe to Foucault's intellectual perspectives and methodologies any defining label (partly because it is impossible to write 'perspective' and 'methodology' in the singular when referring to Foucault). One label that has been consistently attributed to him, and that he just as consistently rejected, is 'structuralist'. In an interview held in 1983, published as 'Structuralism and Post-Structuralism', Foucault claims categorically, 'I have never been a Freudian, I have never been a Marxist and I have never been a structuralist' (*EW ii*, p. 437). And in the preface to the English translation of *The Order of Things*, Foucault writes: 'In France, certain half-witted "commentators" persist in labelling me a "structuralist". I have been unable to get it into their tiny minds that I have used none of the methods, concepts or key terms that characterise structural analysis' (*OT*, p. xv). Despite his objections and negations, Foucault's affinities with this latter term deserve particular attention, especially in the light of his acknowledged debt to the proto-structuralist Dumézil and his proximity to the group of French intellectuals at the centre of structuralist activity. (The differing applications of the 'structuralist' label were such that it is not accurate to term structuralism a 'movement' as such.) Foucault served alongside Roland Barthes, for example, from 1963, as a member of the editorial board of the journal *Critique*, and counted Julia Kristeva and Philippe Sollers, key members of the *Tel Quel* group associated with high structuralism, among his group of interlocutors and collaborators. Structuralism was the philosophical and literary method that rose to prominence in France in the 1960s and 1970s. It wished to ring the definitive death knell of the humanist underpinnings of phenomenology and existentialism, in favour of the rigorous study of systems and signs. These could be linguistic (Saussure's seminal assertion that the relationship between the signifier and the signified is arbitrary, and that language should be studied synchronically rather than diachronically); anthropological (Lévi-Strauss's analyses of systems of kinship); or literary (Roman Jakobson's reading of poetry as a set of formal rules, Barthes's structural analysis of narrative).

The refusal of structuralist analyses to engage with historical context is an obvious point of divergence from Foucault's method, intimately connected as it is with rewriting histories and historicising the apparently transcendental. However, the structuralist agenda of reading literature in order to observe its inner rules, codes and patterns, rather than its content and meaning, *is* consistent with some of Foucault's assertions. His theory of the 'author function' – the idea that we must understand the author's name as a signifier of a set of historical and cultural conditions that led to the production of given ideas, rather than as the nomenclature of an individual genius – echoes Barthes's groundbreaking notion of the 'death of the author' in 1967. Similarly, Foucault attempts to read history without taking account of the agency of personalities, and to observe the operation of discourse without assuming a personal intentionality behind it. Thus, as with almost every other intellectual trend that he encountered, Foucault engaged judiciously with those elements that contributed to his project, but distanced himself from those aspects which ran counter to his primary interests and strategies. Above all, he resisted the constraints of being anchored to an identificatory label.

It is mainly with reference to his work of the 1960s in the 'archaeological' vein that Foucault's concerns can be said to resemble most closely those of structuralism. The Foucaldian method of archaeology was developed in *The Birth of the Clinic* (1963), the subtitle of which is 'An Archaeology of Medical Perception'; but archaeology became most explicitly associated with structuralism in 1966. In this year, Foucault published *The Order of Things*, an attempt to uncover the tacit rules governing the organisation of knowledge at a given historical moment. The book was greeted as a key text of structuralism; indeed, Foucault himself privately described this book as his 'book about signs'.[11] Despite this, *The Order of Things* and, to an even greater extent, the book that followed it, *The Archaeology of Knowledge*, actually use the term 'sign' rather sparingly and tend to focus instead on 'episteme' (in *The Order of Things*) and 'discourse' (in *The Archaeology of Knowledge*), this latter being a term that would interest him throughout the course of his work, but which he uses in the archaeological texts only to mean a set of statements that are made official or authoritative under the governance of a specific set of rules, proper to a given discipline. What this early use of the concept of discourse lacks is a fully formed notion of power – of the way in which 'discursive formations' are intimately involved with institutions and socio-political situations. By the time Foucault comes to write *The Will to Knowledge*, discourse is a much more specific concept, describing the intersection of knowledge and power and the forms of expression and articulation they take in different fields.

Foucault used the term 'archaeology' to designate an analysis of the conditions necessary for a given system of thought to come into being and to impose itself authoritatively. The rules underpinning any system of thought – rules that are not always transparent even to those employing them – are defined as the 'historical unconscious' of the period, or its 'episteme'/'archive'. One of Foucault's aims is to show, via an exploration of the past, the situation of the present. Thus similar underlying 'rules' to the ones that may have allowed the ancient Chinese, according to a fictional text by Borges, to classify animals according to such seemingly bizarre categories as 'fabulous', 'included in the present classification', 'innumerable' and 'drawn with a very fine camelhair brush' (*OT*, p. xvi) still operate today, governing and delimiting our ability to think certain things in certain ways. Of course, to us, the way in which we organise our knowledge does not appear odd and arbitrary like the classification of animals cited above, but reasonable and justified by both scientific method and 'common sense'. However, like Saussure's characterisation of the relationship between the signifier ('dog') and the furry, barking mammal as wholly arbitrary, Foucault's contention is that our most instinctive and automatic assumptions about the truthful and inevitable rules pertaining to the nature of things may well seem, to some future epoch, entirely random and laughable, or else be completely lost to them. Undermining the tyranny of 'common sense' and the lauding of reason may be identified as one of Foucault's principal and unchanging aims.

Archaeology is a history, but it is not a history of things, phenomena or people. It is rather a history of the conditions necessary for given things, phenomena or people to occur. It is an impersonal history and it tends to describe the constellation of the thinkable at a given epochal moment rather than a chronology of the development of thought, making it a rather static-seeming map of epistemology. It is also, however, an internal history – the history of what operates on people to make them think in a certain way, without their being necessarily aware of these forces of influence. It is in this respect that Foucault gets closest in a work like *The Order of Things* to the psychoanalytic method from which elsewhere he will distance himself. The archaeology is psychoanalytically informed because it admits of the possibility of unconscious functioning, even if the unconscious concerned is a collective cultural one rather than the individual's. By 'unconscious', Foucault means hidden, inaccessible rules, codes and beliefs that have effects in the world; but effects which appear as facts of nature. However, it is distinct from psychoanalysis insofar as it does not offer interpretations or propose 'cures' for misguided beliefs based on unconscious phantasy. It simply describes what it uncovers or lays bare, as the metaphor of 'archaeology' would suggest.

Foucault's ultimate rejection of the potential sterility of the archaeological method and its approximation to structuralism occurred, perhaps, in tandem with the reassertion of the imperative for the intellectual to be politically motivated at a grass-roots level. The students' revolts of May 1968, the ensuing workers' general strike, and the climate of unrest and opposition that surrounded them, touched most intellectual figures in France and provided a political and intellectual watershed. Foucault was not present for the events at Nanterre and the Sorbonne in 1968, as he was out of France at the time, occupying a university post in Tunisia. However, he was very sensitised to the spirit of the time. In 1966, he had supported student strike action in Tunisia and, once back in France and in post at Vincennes University in 1969, he was arrested for showing solidarity with his students during their occupation of university buildings. The aftermath of the student insurrections created a strong oppositional political sensibility among French intellectuals of the generation. This expressed itself in an increasingly vociferous criticism of American neo-colonialist foreign policy and institutionalised racism in France. It also found expression at a more local level. For the Marxist thinker Henri Lefebvre, the everyday became the sphere in which the political was most at stake. For Foucault too, the revolt against institutions heralded by '68 broadened the definition of politics, such that 'subjects like psychiatry, confinement and the medicalisation of a population have become political problems'.[12] With this in mind, the mere identification of signs and their functions within systems may have begun to seem redundant or sterile. Foucault's engagement with the everyday political questions he identified operated at the practical as well as the intellectual level. In 1971, he became involved, along with his friend and lover Daniel Defert, with the Groupe d'Information sur les prisons, a group of intellectuals and ex-prisoners seeking to establish information on conditions in jail and investigate prisoners' complaints of mistreatment. Their aim was not to campaign for reform, but to encourage and empower prisoners to protest on their own behalf. He was also active in the Groupe d'Information sur la santé, a health information group set up by doctors, which became involved in political struggles for legalised abortion and patients' rights. Around the same time, the Front Homosexuel d'Action Révolutionnaire (FHAR) came into being, an informal and highly libidinous group that clustered around the charismatic figure of Guy Hocquenghem, author of *Homosexual Desire* (1972). Foucault declined to become involved with the group, however, expressing his mistrust of the value of 'sexual liberation', a conviction that would find theoretical expression in *The Will to Knowledge*. Indeed, Foucault seldom described himself as having a 'gay identity', mistrusting the notion of identity despite his interest, particularly towards the end of his life, in the possibilities offered by gay subcultures for community formation and new relational organisations. Moreover, while refusing to join any liberation movement, Foucault none the less contributed articles to France's first radical gay publication *Gai pied* and, allegedly, thought up its title.[13] He also, as David Macey has pointed out, expressed support for the more assimilationist or 'homophile' organisation *Arcadie*, by delivering an address at one of its annual conferences. While continuing to be suspicious of liberationist discourses in general, then, Foucault nevertheless 'floated', giving generously of his time, solidarity and intellectual input without feeling the need to become a member of either group or form a fixed affiliation.

The broad shift heralded by '68 thus brought together theory and activism and provided a focus and a political justification for Foucault's investigations of institutions and sexuality. While Barthes and Kristeva continued to produce structuralist theory well into the 1970s and 1980s, Foucault retained the interest in history so prominent in the archaeologies, but strengthened his commitment to producing a critical history of power or, more properly, went on to explore the political and intellectual insights and opportunities of the method he would term 'genealogy', which allow for an analysis of the effects of the institutional and resistant operations of power within systems of thought, as well as a synchronic description of the conditions of their emergence.

Nietzsche, genealogy, influence

Foucault's 'genealogical' works (namely *Discipline and Punish* and *The Will to Knowledge*) are heavily indebted to the German philosopher Friedrich Nietzsche. Foucault's widely cited essay, 'Nietzsche, Genealogy, History' (1971), is a close textual reading of Nietzsche's work, an *explication de texte* in the French tradition, written for a collection of essays in honour of Jean Hyppolite. The essay sets out to elaborate Nietzsche's notion of genealogy, but it does not offer very much in the way of insight into Foucault's own particular adaptations and applications of Nietzsche's method. Foucault's interest in this thinker dates back to the early 1950s, inspired by his reading of Bataille and Blanchot, and predates the more widespread reception of Nietzsche in French philosophy.[14] His fascination with Nietzsche, which he has described as a 'point of rupture' (*EW ii*, p. 438) in his thinking, may account in part for his progressive and intensified dissociation from phenomenological perspectives between the early works on insanity and the later works on knowledge, literature and the disciplines. Already in *The Order of Things*, Foucault had stated that Nietzsche 'marks the threshold beyond which contemporary philosophy can begin thinking again; and he will no doubt continue for a long while to dominate its advance' (*OT*, p. 373). That this statement comes towards the end of the long book, such that the 'way forward' offered by a Nietzschean perspective seems to extend beyond the end of Foucault's analysis in that work, may not be coincidental. Foucault's debt to Nietzsche's ideas, then, is considerable, even though for several years critics tended to overlook its importance. In 1979, Allan Megill stated that 'Nietzsche has been the single most important influence on Foucault's work.'[15] A few years later, key works by Alan Sheridan[16] and by Charles Lemert and Garth Gillan[17] brought serious attention to Foucault's Nietzschean agenda; and in his recent *Nietzsche and Postmodernism*, Dave Robinson affirms Foucault's part in giving Nietzsche's work a life beyond its own historical period, going so far as to claim that 'Michel Foucault [. . .] was probably the first post-war philosopher to take Nietzsche seriously as a thinker.'[18]

Nietzsche offered a way of thinking about history that was in direct opposition to the popular Hegelian dialectical model and the currents of thought that were inspired by it (e.g. Marxism). Nietzsche sought to uncover, via the observation of localised and relational, rather than continuous, historical operations of power, the installation of 'false universals', interested ideologies that are made to pass as neutral and naturally occurring 'facts'. If we observe Nietzsche's definition of the Enlightenment as the moment at which 'clever animals invented knowledge',[19] and his observation that 'It was the most arrogant and mendacious moment of "universal history"',[20] we begin to see how Nietzsche's irreverent response to Kant's question 'What is Enlightenment?' may have given Foucault a methodological handle on a central question that would occupy him throughout his corpus: 'How does one elaborate a history of rationality?' (*EW ii*, p. 439). Nietzsche's concern to call into question the nineteenth century's prevalent discourse of progress and improvement through the lauding of rationality offered Foucault a context for his attempts to call 'truth' into question and to catalogue the invention of forms of knowledge and the conditions of their crystallisation into institutions of authority. The guiding principles of this project underlie not only the later genealogical critiques but much of Foucault's *œuvre*. Nietzsche's key technique of calling the obvious into question was adapted by Foucault for specific and applied purposes: for the close interrogation of given fields of knowledge.

As well as adapting his methods, Foucault often employs a technique of imitation with regard to Nietzsche's style. Strategic imitation is a typical Foucaldian device, used both in the service of parodic critique and in endorsement or tribute. For example, he echoes and extends one of Nietzsche's most (in)famous claims: where Nietzsche proclaims the death of God, Foucault announces at the end of *The Order of Things* the death of man, whereby that historical construction, the human being, is likened to a face drawn in the sand and about to be erased by the movement of the tide washing over it. Perhaps the most explicit nod to the German philosopher is found in the naming of the first volume of *The History of Sexuality* as *The Will to Knowledge*, an acknowledgement of the centrality to Foucault's thought of Nietzsche's concept of the Will to Power, an idea developed from the German philosopher's reading of Schopenhauer, and describing the constant state of struggle that characterises human desire and endeavour. All forms of 'knowledge' and 'truth' are merely the triumphant version of events that has succeeded in emerging from the perpetual struggle of ideas and ideologies that characterises our way of interacting. If the outcome of given historical power struggles had been different, the notion of 'the truth' we would have inherited might now look radically different.

However, certain critics have argued that Foucault's precise use of the term 'genealogy' may not be synonymous with Nietzsche's. Gary Gutting, for example, has pointed out that Nietzsche's use of this term signifies less of a systematic method than Foucault's, informed by very little historical research, and often relying on personal opinions and observations.[21] It is also more interested in psychological explanations of phenomena and in the psychological traits that may persist throughout history. Gutting has also pointed out that many of Nietzsche's ideas – for example those on women and on species degeneration due to racial mixing – appear rebarbative to modern readers, and are certainly not part of Foucault's own worldview. While this perspective may have some validity, we must not underestimate the extent to which the positions taken up by Nietzsche, like those adopted by Foucault, are often strategically employed with the purpose of critiquing prevalent contemporary belief systems. The playful, ludic and indeed often ironic aspects of both thinkers' work are essential to an understanding of their 'critique of reason'. A good example would be Nietzsche's outburst regarding the damaging qualities of Christianity: 'I call Christianity the one great curse, the one enormous and innermost perversion, the one great instinct of revenge for which no means are too venomous, too underhand and too petty – I call it the one immortal blemish of mankind.'[22] Now, if we are to read this statement 'straight', it does indeed seem, as Gutting would argue, that Nietzsche interprets and *evaluates* such phenomena as Christianity according to his own capricious and personal perspective. However, a more productive reading technique, employable both for Foucault and Nietzsche, may lie in an awareness of the extent to which the two thinkers tend to use a given discourse *against itself*, deploying it citationally for parodic effect. Nietzsche's rant here apes ironically the moralistic tenor of a preacher in the pulpit, railing against wrongdoers' sin and 'perversion' (that favoured term which the nineteenth century would shift from the lexicon of religion to that of sexology). Nietzsche uses the very language of the discourse he is critiquing to lambast it, to mock it. This technique is one that Foucault would borrow *from* Nietzsche and use to great effect throughout his work, a fact suggested explicitly when Foucault describes Nietzsche's writings as 'strange, witty, cheeky texts' – antidotes to the dry and 'classical' propositions of Descartes, Kant, Hegel and Husserl,[23] much as Gilles Deleuze finds Foucault's texts imbued with 'an increasing sense of joy and gaiety' capable of provoking 'unexpected laughter'.[24]

Nietzsche's genealogy has as its driving motivation, then, the wish to rethink history, refusing the contemporary, post-Enlightenment, nineteenth-century ideal of the grand narrative of history as that of the triumph of human progress. For Nietzsche, the idea that the epoch in which he lived marked the high point of civilised achievement was a fiction to be debunked. Nietzsche counters the idea of the progress of modern times with the contention that there is an essential, enduring (one might say universal, despite Nietzsche's strategic dislike of this concept), psychological factor driving humankind through its different historical moments: the aforementioned Will to Power. This is a drive for individual transcendence. In this model, conflict is inevitable, but it is a conflict that is productive and re-energising rather than negative. Nietzsche's rather warlike philosophical discourse can be seen to have influenced the militaristic language of Foucault's late textuality. In the latter, 'battle plans' (*plans de bataille*),[25] and 'strategies' (*stratégies*)[26] are found in abundance. In Nietzsche's work, some universals (the omnipresence and inevitability of the Will to Power) sit uneasily alongside the more proto-'constructivist' idea that certain individuals can forge their own identities. (These individuals are described as the controversial *Übermensch* or superior human being capable of overcoming for himself the common conditions of his culture [the gender pronouns are deliberate here – Nietzsche doesn't consider the *Überfrau*].) Late Foucaldian writings are also interested in this notion of self-construction via an ethics of personal *askesis*, but the elitist notion of the *Übermensch* is absent. However, as I shall discuss in the penultimate and final chapters, Foucault's focus on the figure of the free Greek male as exemplary subject of self-stylisation has laid him open to charges of elitism and gender blindness too.

A specifically Foucaldian genealogy is, then, a history that, like Nietzsche's, is suspicious of grand narratives and seismic shifts, single causes for historical change and value-laden teleologies of progress. It is a history of the small and multiple changes that lead to alterations in trends of thinking and operating in any given epoch. For example, Foucault argues that the making of the modern sexual subject was the result of no single legal, socio-economic or medical 'development', but rather the simultaneous coming into being of an infinitesimal number of arbitrary but co-existing factors: the rise of clinic-based psychology, Freud's machinations in *fin-de-siècle* Vienna, the implementation of methods for monitoring adolescent bodies, the proliferation of techniques for eliciting confessions, etc. A second unique feature of Foucaldian genealogy, distinct from the Nietzschean kind, is the central focus on the body. Foucault insists that the human body is the locus in and over which power operates. Each epoch has its way of producing the kinds of bodies that conform to its expectations and needs. Thus, in *The Birth of the Clinic*, an early archaeological text that makes some prescient genealogical gestures towards an analytics of power, 'truths' about disease can be elicited by means of a very particular medical gaze at and within the dead body. And later, in *Discipline and Punish*, the visibly tortured body of the seventeenth century gives way to the rigorously disciplined body of the modern prisoner, soldier, asylum inmate or schoolchild, in which obedience and regimented control are internalised. Despite the differences between them, Foucault borrows from Nietzsche not only the method of genealogy as a tool with which to oppose a history of rational progress and dialectical thought, but also a rhetorical writing style that is polyvocal, jubilant, ludic and always asking us to question whose discourse is being evoked and how seriously we are to take it.

Disrupting disciplines

One can argue, then, that the development of a method of genealogy via his readings of Nietzsche enabled Foucault to escape more effectively and productively from the humanism of phenomenology than his ambivalent flirting with a synchronic model of history (archaeology) had done; and also to escape the hated label of structuralist. The idea that Foucault's work did not overlap perfectly with the agenda of structuralism, and that, where his method could be described as structuralist, it was not properly a 'structuralism of structures', was acknowledged by some contemporaries, including Jean Piaget. Piaget termed Foucault's work, conversely, 'a structuralism *without* structures'.[27] Foucault was not alone of his generation in refusing to align himself wholeheartedly with the structuralism that had influenced him, but that ultimately he had found wanting. Thinkers such as Lacan, Deleuze, Félix Guattari and Jacques Derrida, like Foucault, had welcomed structuralism's rejection of the unified, meaning-making subject (the Cartesian *cogito*), but also found difficulty with the notion that literature, culture, the psyche etc. are governed *always and only* by inherent structural rules and the insistence that both historical context and content are irrelevant. For this reason, the term 'post-structuralist' is often applied to these thinkers. One should not, however, make the mistake of thinking that Foucault shared identical affinities or guiding methods with other post-structuralist thinkers. He distanced himself from both Lacanian psychoanalysis and Derridean deconstruction, challenging the Freudian epistemology of the former and accusing the latter of privileging a critic-centred authority: in arguing that there is nothing outside the text, Derrida promotes a 'pedagogy that gives [. . .] to the master's voice the limitless sovereignty that allows it to restate the text indefinitely' (*EW ii*, p. 416).

Thus Foucault's discomfort with the label of structuralist and his eclectic methodology, drawing on Marx, Dumézil, Canguilhem, Nietzsche and others, make it difficult to categorise his thought in any meaningful way. This may be precisely what Foucault intended. As well as flirting with various methodologies and currents of thought, he similarly enjoyed productive but fluid affiliations with several academic disciplines (including psychology, history, philosophy and French literary studies), refusing to commit himself wholly to

any of them, and seeking to challenge and renovate their methods and ide-
ologies where possible. The titles of several recent books, including *Foucault:
Historian or Philosopher*,[28] *Between Genealogy and Epistemology: Psychology,
Politics and Knowledge in the Thought of Michel Foucault*,[29] and *Foucault, Health
and Medicine*,[30] bear witness to the ongoing difficulty for critics of 'placing'
Foucault.

His contribution to history is particularly influential and controversial. As
well as being strongly influenced by Nietzsche, Foucault's work shares certain
affinities with the *Annales* movement inaugurated by Lucien Febvre and Marc
Bloch, in so far as both the *Annalistes*' and Foucault's projects are concerned
with expanding the scope of historical endeavour in order to question commonplaces about the everyday and the contingent.[31] However, where they part
company is with regard to the vital place accorded to power in Foucault's work.
In 'Return to History', Foucault argues that history itself is a bourgeois invention, a narrative designed and constructed to present the domination of the
higher classes as inevitable, and therefore to 'prove' the impossibility of revolution, since the dominant order appears to have originated with the dawn
of time and to reflect the natural order of things. He argues that the 'calling
and role of history now must be reconsidered if history is to be detached from
the ideological system in which it originated and developed' (*EW ii*, p. 423).
Foucault weds philosophy with historical method (outraging many traditional
historians in the process), in order to explore the questions: 'How is it that the
human subject took itself as the object of possible knowledge? Through what
forms of rationality and historical conditions? And finally, at what price?' (*EW
ii*, p. 444). Moreover, as a self-described student of the 'history of the present'
(*DP*, p. 31), he sought to denaturalise our relationship to the conditions of
our social existence in the present by critically examining the past. In Foucault's account, the present is not the triumph of historical progress, but one
outcome of a series of complex and discontinuous forces and influences over
time. His unconventional methods have influenced a subsequent generation of
cultural and literary historiographers, including the 'New Historicists', whose
break with the ahistorical aspects of 'theory' in search of a re-examination
of historical and sociological specificity is often attributed to the influence of
Foucault (a fact which has a certain irony, given that it is Foucault's philosophical and polemic qualities that have tended to alienate mainstream academic
historians).

Similarly, Foucault's contribution to the academic study of politics and government has been an important one, with the development in his late work
(from the 1970s until his death) of a rich analysis of 'governmentality'. In a
lecture which takes this neologism as its title,[32] Foucault sketches a genealogy

of forms of government, taking as its starting point the sixteenth century, during which there emerged a concern with an 'art of government' and numerous treatises on this subject. This concern arose in response to the model of sovereign power proposed in Machiavelli's *The Prince*, from which Foucault draws primary material. According to Machiavelli's treatise on leadership, the prince should lead via a transcendental relation of power over his people and territory, whether acquired by force, treaty or inheritance. The prince's role is to ensure his continued domination over the territory he has acquired from his external position of control. The concept of governmentality, then, emerges in contradistinction to this transcendental model of rule. The anti-Machiavellian commentators on the art of government argued, according to Foucault, that government should not remain in this position of monolithic exteriority to the governed territory and people. Rather, the art of governing involves 'multiplicity and immanence' rather than 'transcendent singularity'.[33] Its aim is the most effective functioning of the state, or 'the pursuit of the perfection and intensification of the processes which it directs'; such that 'the instruments of government, instead of being laws, now come to be a range of multiform tactics'.[34] This tactical organisation of society increases as a result of waning belief in the sovereignty of the leader – his direct link to God – and strengthened belief in the state as a self-regulating body.

Modern society, Foucault argues, operates according to the principle of governmentality, the history of which he has traced. In modern society, governmentality consists of a tripartite set of linked concerns: 'sovereignty–discipline–government'. Foucault's concept is designed to counter notions of state power as unidirectional (the negative view of power in which it operates from the top down by oppression) as proposed by Marxian analysts, or as static. Regulation (of bodies, populations, children, citizens, sexualities) occurs by means of networks of strategic power relations, such as the ones described in *Discipline and Punish* and *The Will to Knowledge*. The concepts of disciplinary power and bio-power explored respectively in these two works are strategic elements of governmentality.

Foucault's writing on government and the state contributes to his complex and not always consistent ideas about the status of the social subject. While his ubiquitous critique of individual autonomous identity can seem to stand as a rejection of the ideal of individualistic neo-liberalism that pervades late twentieth-century Western culture, Foucault's tendency in his late writings to oppose individual practices of freedom to an idea of state resembles, at moments, a politics of liberalism. However, rather than offering a liberal position, as Lois McNay has pointed out, for Foucault 'liberal thought is treated as an exemplary model of the dilemma that lies at the heart of the problem of social control in modern societies, namely the possibility of government without intervention'.[35]

Similar questions of power and citizenship – which center around the difficult relationship between *subjectivity* and *subjectivation* – are addressed in the series of lectures delivered in 1975–6 and recently published in English as *Society Must be Defended*. Foucault argues that 'in order to conduct a concrete analysis of power relations, one would have to abandon the juridical notion of sovereignty' (*EW i*, p. 59), because this model is overly simplistic in its assumption of the individual citizen as subject of rights and powers. Following his later model of power as force which operates relationally, multidirectionally and with plural effects, Foucault sets out to ask if it is useful to think of power relations in society along analogous lines with operations of war. This leads him to the original and provocative statement that 'politics is war by other means' (*SMD*, p. 69), gesturing towards a fruitful reading of class struggle and racial tensions, which are habitually subsumed under the operations of peacetime bio-politics – the organisation of the population by insidious and multivalent means. Although, as has been pointed out in recent criticism,[36] Foucault's discussion of race is strangely silent on the subject of colonialism, the analyses of 'state racism' undertaken in this series of lectures are, while problematic in certain ways, still particularly relevant for scholars considering the politics of multiculturalism and questions of ethnicity today.

While he contributed to numerous disciplines, then, it is perhaps most helpful to see Foucault's major achievement as a disruption of their traditional methods. Foucault's disruption of disciplinary commonplaces and undermining of accepted wisdom is perhaps best exemplified by the methodology he applied in a lecture given in 1964 (published in 1967 as 'Nietzsche, Freud, Marx') to a re-reading of the philosophical contributions of these three 'great thinkers'. Foucault takes thinkers commonly read for the 'deep structures' assumed to underlie their thought – the Will to Power under the moral ideal (Nietzsche); the social force under the commodity fetish (Marx); and primordial trauma beneath the symptom (Freud) – and radically reinterprets what it is that these iconic names actually reveal. All three, claims Foucault, bring to light not the depths of truth, but rather the fiction at the heart of depth claims and the extent to which interpretation has already been placed on that which may, at first, appear as original material awaiting primary interpretation. Thus, depth itself re-emerges as 'an absolutely superficial secret' (*EW ii*, p. 273). Nietzsche's philosophy is shown to demonstrate that there is no signified under the signifier, since the ruling classes *invent* language in order to impose an interpretation. Marx is concerned with an *interpretation* of relations of production, not with the relations themselves. And Freud's psychoanalytic theory is shown to reveal the retroactively constructed *fantasy* of a cause of trauma, not a traumatic event itself.

Foucault, then, is an intellectual iconoclast. This iconoclasm and disregard for traditional intellectual limits and boundaries is reflected in the academic title he assumed when appointed to a Chair at the prestigious Collège de France in 1970. 'Professor of the History of Systems of Thought' designated excellence in an original field of inquiry that defied easy disciplinary classification. In 1984, Foucault designated his life-long field of inquiry and guiding objective as follows:

> My objective for more than 25 years has been to sketch out a history of the different ways in our culture that humans develop knowledge about themselves: economics, biology, psychiatry, medicine and penology. The main point is not to accept this knowledge at face value but to analyze these so-called sciences as very specific 'truth games' related to specific techniques that human beings use to understand themselves.
>
> (*TS*, pp. 17–18)

Foucault's intellectual hybridity and refusal of established or sclerotic disciplinary affiliations make him a prescient forerunner of the contemporary Anglo-American trend for interdisciplinarity. The idea that by working across disciplinary boundaries, the blind spots and limits of each system of knowledge are brought to light and their ideologies relativised, is a profoundly Foucaldian one. Similarly, always concerned with showing up how the apparent humanitarianism of reason disguised techniques of oppression and marginalisation, Foucault argued against historians and philosophers who write neutrally, apolitically, 'as if we were afraid to conceive of the *Other* in the time of our own thought' (*AK*, p. 13). That he was able to pursue these disruptive, revisionist and seemingly anarchical intellectual projects in the traditionalist university system of France in 1970 is all the more remarkable. However, it is also true that Foucault became increasingly attracted to the intellectual life of the USA in the late 1970s, having given a series of visiting lectures at both Berkeley and Stanford. This interest in American culture also extended to his exploration of its gay scene – Christopher Street and its environs in New York City and the Castro District of San Francisco. American gay communities seemed to offer pleasurable and relational possibilities not found in France, and his observations of SM clubs and bathhouse cultures there would inspire his late utopian writings on the pleasures that might be realised if the disciplinary regime of 'sexuality' could be overcome (as I shall explore in Chapter 7).

Ultimately, then, while it is important to be aware of the intellectual and political currents which coloured Foucault's trajectory and influenced his work, one is also left with the unavoidable impression that primarily he remained a maverick thinker, uncompromising and controversial: seeking to throw into question, rather than contribute to, the fashionable intellectual movements and methods of his day and to infuse them always with a vital and unconventional perspective.

Chapter 2

Works: madness and medicine

I had been mad enough to study reason; I was reasonable enough to study madness.

Michel Foucault

The History of Madness

Foucault's earliest research interests and publications focused on the institutionalisation of medicine, particularly psychiatry in the nineteenth century, in tandem with a fascination with the transgressive potential of madness as an artistic and political force. As I suggested in Chapter 1, Foucault's opus is characterised by a tension between an interest in experience and subjectivity on the one hand, and a devastating critique of these concepts on the other. It is in his early work on madness that the concern with experience – a methodology haunted by something resembling phenomenology – is most visible.

Foucault wished to write a revisionist history of mental illness that would upend the commonplace received view regarding the liberalisation of the treatment of the mad with the birth of modern psychiatry. His investment in this topic and the perspectives from which he approaches it are ambiguous and, potentially, contradictory. Having read philosophy at university, Foucault's interest then turned to the discipline of psychology, and in 1952 he was awarded a diploma in psychopathology after studying under Jean Delay at the Institut de Psychologie. From there, he would go on to gain clinical experience working at the Parisian mental asylum of Saint-Anne, though he did not return to university to complete the training that would have allowed him to practise psychiatry. So, to some extent, Foucault's writings must have stemmed from his experience of working in the role of mental health professional and his first-hand observation of the 'mad'. However, conversely, Foucault suggests in the preface to the first edition of his *History of Madness* that 'madness' will be the *subjective* rather than *objective* viewpoint of the history. He hints that his critique of the history of madness will be written to articulate the historically silenced voice of the mad, rather than from the point of view of the psychiatric professional, and suggests also that his history of psychology and psychiatry emerged as an incidental by-product of this 'reconstitution of [the] experience of madness' (*HM*, p. xxxiv). It is striking (and I shall say more about this later) that most of the primary material for Foucault's theorisation of madness consists of the writings of authors who have been psychiatric patients, such as Nerval and Roussel, rather than 'ordinary' case notes of less distinguished patients, such as would be seen in a work produced within the discipline of psychology or another social science, or indeed within a more traditional history of the mental health professions.

Biographers have suggested that Foucault's own rumoured experiences of depressive episodes and suicidal tendencies as a young man may have played a part in his passionate interest in the subject of psychiatry;[1] It has also been posited that his lifelong critique of medicine and its power structures stemmed from the young Michel's resistance to pressure to follow in his father's footsteps and pursue a career as a physician.[2] However, as stated in Chapter 1, the method of psycho-biography is not one that I shall pursue in this book. Rather, I shall argue that the difficulties and challenges of reading the *History of Madness* can best be appreciated by bearing in mind Foucault's constant intellectual vacillation between a fascination with the power of trangressive subjectivity on the one hand, and the desire to rewrite a history devoid of human agency on the other – agendas that are, if not impossible to reconcile, then certainly in tension with each other.

Foucault wrote several works on madness and the mental health disciplines, some of which have not been translated into other languages, or have had only a limited reception and influence. These include *Maladie mentale et personnalité* (1954), *Maladie mentale et psychologie* (1966), and his comprehensive and erudite introduction to Binswanger's *Dream and Existence* (1954). Foucault's long study *Folie et déraison: histoire de la folie à l'âge classique* (1961) was translated into English in very abridged form in 1965 as *Madness and Civilization: A History of Insanity in the Age of Reason*. Not until 2006 did Routledge bring out a full English translation of the *History*, edited and translated by Jean Khalfa.[3]

As is the case with many of Foucault's historiographical works, the historical period covered in this work is vast. It traces the discourses of reason and unreason from the Middle Ages to the present day. The specific term Foucault uses for madness – *folie* – is the French word for 'folly', which can encompass more easily than the English translation – 'madness' – both the wise idiocy of the Shakespearian fool and the concept of insanity in the modern clinical sense. The shades of meaning of both are thus allowed to co-exist and remain in play throughout Foucault's consideration. The central organising principle of Foucault's argument is that madness and reason have been progressively separated and estranged from each other throughout history, and particularly in modern times, with the result that madness – as psychopathology rather than folly – appears as a 'truth' to be diagnosed and cured by the scientific disciplines. Foucault speaks of an 'act of scission' (*MC*, xii) that created this artificial distinction. This act of scission takes the form of a discourse that silences the voice of the mad, privileging instead the voice of the 'expert':

> As for a common language, there is no such thing; or rather, there is no such thing any longer; the constitution of madness as a mental illness at the end of the eighteenth century, affords the evidence of a broken dialogue, posits the separation as already effected, and thrusts into oblivion all those stammered, imperfect words without fixed syntax in which the exchange between madness and reason was made. The language of psychiatry, which is a monologue of reason about madness, has been established only on the basis of such a silence. I have not tried to write the history of that language, but rather the archaeology of that silence.
>
> (*MC*, p. xii)

Foucault's last point here offers a useful distinction between history and archaeology as methods that are shaped by the subject matter they purport to treat. Linguistic utterances – the articulated, the known, the conscious – would have a history, an authorised and authoritative narrative. A silence, on the other hand, would require an archaeology to bring it to light, a historical method that uncovers what has been forgotten, or what lies in the gaps between the points that are remembered.

The *History of Madness* posits that madness has been understood according to four distinct belief systems in the West. In the Middle Ages, it was considered a holy mystery, but a part of the vast panoply of human experience. In the Renaissance, it was seen as an ironic form of special reason, which laid bare the nonsense of the world. Madmen were at once tragic and comic: 'madness and madmen become major figures, in their ambiguity: menace and mockery, the dizzying unreason of the world, and the feeble ridicule of men' (*MC*, p. 11). The special role played by the mad in the Renaissance, according to Foucault, was to embody a human drama – the potential unreason to which any of the population may become susceptible – and their otherness appeared as a plausible facet of the human condition. This set of ideas is crystallised in the image of the Ship of Fools: a group of madmen set adrift from society, not only as outcasts, but also as pilgrims, in search of their reason and, by extension, the reason of the world. The mad were society's representatives in the non-social realm; they forged a link between order and chaos.

In these early periods, then, according to Foucault, madness had a *relationship* with sanity. Pre-modernity posited them as alternative ways of relating to the underlying absurdity of the world, rather than *opposing* them within a binary system, as healthy and correct on the one hand or aberrant and sick on the other, as today. Moreover, madness in pre-modernity carried eschatological implications. The 'wisdom of fools' suggested in the images and texts that Foucault cites presages 'both the reign of Satan and the end of the world; ultimate bliss and supreme punishment; omnipotence on earth and the eternal fall' (*MC*, p. 19). Madness stands as the threat to the world, understood as God's creation, and the order it imposes. Since the threat posed by madness was felt to operate at a theological, rather than just a social, level in the Renaissance, it was therefore potentially the concern of all. Foucault risks elevating madness in his discussion of this period to a disruptive principle of anarchic victory over hierarchy and order, delivered via man with 'his weaknesses, dreams and illusions' (*MC*, p. 23). Quasi- and proto-Nietzschean here, Foucault's pre-modern madman effectively threatens to dethrone God.

According to Foucault, the major shift in the conceptualisation of madness dates from the middle of the seventeenth century. At this historical moment, the madman ceased to be a figure of tragi-comic wisdom, in confrontation with the cosmos, and became a hospital patient, contained in 'enormous houses of confinement' (*MC*, p. 35). Foucault argues that madhouses in the 'classical age' (the term he uses throughout his corpus to mean the seventeenth and eighteenth centuries)[4] were not yet medical asylums but 'semi-juridical' institutions. In addition to the mad, the poor, the sick, and the unemployed of both sexes found themselves segregated from mainstream society by this structure. In Foucault's cynical reading, it offered a dual response to the fluctuations of the European economy, both containing the unproductive and potentially restive in times of financial crisis and *making* them productive in times of high employment, in the form of cheap labour. This move marked the point at which madness was first viewed as a civic problem, as impinging on the financial stability of the nation, in a historical imaginary that was developing the duty to work as a moral prescription.

A second fundamental change noted is that of the dehumanisation of the mad during the period of the great confinement. Where once madness had been intrinsic to the perceived nature of the human condition, suddenly madness became comprehensible as the trace of animality in the human being. The madman gives in to his passions, rather than being governed by reason. This gives rise to the earliest form of psychiatry, to the invention for the first time of taxonomies of madness, the labelling of forms that the exercise of the passions could take: mania, melancholia, hysteria and hypochondria.

With the dawning of modernity, madness became properly the object of the science of psychiatry, which would increasingly aim to denude itself of religious or moral considerations and become a therapeutic discipline. Where once, Foucault argues, unreason was understood as a *special form of* reason, modern psychiatry establishes instead a discourse *about* madness, which articulates itself at the price of unreason's silence. Foucault's history of psychiatry is revisionist to the extent that it questions the commonly held view that psychiatry marked a humanitarian turn in the treatment of the mentally ill. Foucault gives us several examples of the well-worn notion of 'psychiatrist as philanthropist', including the famous story of Philippe Pinel, the maker of early French psychiatry or 'alienism', releasing the chained-up prisoners of the Bicêtre in 1793, and the case of Samuel Tuke, a British reformer who founded a Quaker asylum for the mad in a pastoral English idyll around the same time. The traditional history of psychiatry has taken these figures as its heroes: men of science who replaced superstitious fear with reason, and physical confinement with sympathetic therapeutic treatment. For Foucault, however, this perception is only a very partial one. Foucault shows how Tuke's treatment was informed by a religious morality and involved making the mad person 'feel morally responsible for everything in him that may disturb morality and society' (*MC* p. 234). In this way, 'Tuke created an asylum where he substituted for the free terror of madness the stifling anguish of responsibility' (*MC* p. 234). We see here a beautiful example of Foucault's important gesture of re-evaluating historical received wisdom, and reinterpreting history through a politicised lens sensitised to the perspective of the other.

Tuke's methods for normalising the sick included hosting tea parties at which patients were required to behave with consummate social politeness and etiquette. Generally, according to reports, these parties were harmonious and enjoyable occasions. For Foucault, however, this is not the sign of a successful ethical or humanitarian treatment of madness. Far from it, as it involves a moralistic silencing of the other's articulation of his/her truth: 'the madman is obliged to objectify himself in the eyes of reason as the perfect stranger, that is, as the man whose strangeness does not reveal itself. The city of reason welcomes him only with this qualification and at the price of this surrender to anonymity' (*MC*, p. 237). The expectation that the mad should learn and assimilate the codes and values of bourgeois society, and never allow themselves to deviate visibly from its norms, led, according to Foucault, to a regime in which the mad, while no longer physically chained, were just as constrained as ever by their imprisonment in a 'moral world': 'Something had been born which was no longer repression but authority' (*MC*, p. 238). This is an important gesture, as it pre-figures Foucault's later exposition of the model of disciplinary power in *Discipline and Punish*: a form of internalised 'authority'. Even in the case of Pinel's clinic, in which religious views were more likely to be viewed through a rational medical lens as symptoms of delirium, rather than as an organising moral principle of rehabilitation, Foucault argues that the asylum became, under this same regime of authority, 'a religious domain without religion' (*MC*, p. 244). The authority became embodied, as modern psychiatric medicine developed apart from an explicit concern with morality, in the figure of the doctor, the specialist, the expert. Foucault claims that it was Tuke's and Pinel's purchase on moral authority as doctors (as medicine increasingly gained social status and respectability) that led to them being the ones to treat the mad, rather than any specialist knowledge they possessed, since the treatments used at the beginning of the nineteenth century were not medical in nature. The 'creation' of mental illness as a health-care specialism in the early-twentieth century justified the continued authority of doctors over the mad once a medical, rather than moral, model of treatment was adopted.

Even psychoanalysis, the so-called 'talking cure', does not, Foucault argues, offer a convincing exception to his contention that the authority of medicine silenced the mad. Although he removed the mad from the confines of the asylum to the accessible space of the consulting room, Freud extended the powers of the asylum to the maximum, such that 'by an inspired short-circuit, alienation becomes disalienating because, in the doctor, it becomes a subject' (*MC*, p. 264). By this, Foucault means that psychoanalysis, through techniques of diagnosis and the subjection of the patient to a position within a pre-established discourse of psychopathology, refuses – is unable – to hear 'the voices of unreason' (*MC*, p. 264), and instead converts it into the articulation of a *symptom*: the surface cry of a previously repressed trauma that must be interpreted within the psychoanalytic grid of meaning.

The conclusion of *Madness and Civilisation* seeks to identify where, in modernity, the voice of unreason, untrammelled by psychopathological discourse, may be heard. The answer, it seems, is in art and literature:

> Since the end of the eighteenth century, the life of unreason no longer manifests itself except in the lightning-flash of works such as those of Hölderlin, of Nietzsche, or of Artaud – forever irreducible to those alienations that can be cured, resisting by their own strengths that gigantic moral imprisonment which we are in the habit of calling, doubtless by antiphrasis, the liberation of the insane by Pinel and Tuke.
>
> (*MC*, p. 264)

Foucault's central notion – that modernity involved a silencing of the voice of madness that would otherwise offer an alternative wisdom – is an interesting but problematic one. It is hard to see how something so elusive as 'the voice of madness' may offer any sort of concerted political discourse with which to challenge the bourgeois mainstream. For one thing, it is not easy to see how a non-rational experience or previously silenced voice may be harnessed for politically disruptive purposes, since madness must stand in contradistinction to any organised rebellion or political agenda – a point argued forcefully by Gary Gutting who is dismissive of Foucault's romanticisation of madness.[5] In the chapter of this book dedicated to Foucault's writing on avant-garde literature, I shall show how his interest in 'mad' authors, such as the ones he names in the quotation above, allows him to form a theory of writing and transgression that may thematise this resistance slightly more convincingly in the realm of the politics of art than in the realm of the socio-political. On the other hand, given the weight of suspicion that accrued to unreason in the writings of post-Enlightenment French philosophers and medics such as Maine de Biran, as well as alienists and doctors like Pinel, Esquirol and Monneret (with whose work Foucault was very familiar), his analysis of its dissident potential offers a strangely seductive critical reading, showing up the silenced fear subtending rational discourse, the fantasy against which reason asserts itself. To be fair, Foucault himself was volubly ambivalent about the feasibility of the project he proposed, sometimes writing confidently about a primal experience of madness, while at other times acknowledging the difficulty of expressing this experience at all adequately. In his original preface he writes:

> To write the history of madness will therefore mean making a structural study of the historical ensemble – notions, institutions, judicial and police measures, scientific concepts – which hold captive a madness whose wild state can never be reconstituted; but in the absence of that inaccessible primitive purity, the structural study must go back to the decision that both bound and separated reason and madness.
>
> (*HM*, p. xxxiii)

Rosi Braidotti has argued, following Gilles Deleuze, that Foucault's account of madness is an important one, since it functions as an at once impossible and crucial category, a void in which non-meaning circulates infinitely, all the while allowing for the production of potential meanings. Thus it is an empty container that fulfils the structural function of disruption, without any strategic content or conscious volition.[6]

In many ways, Foucault's 'defence' of madness can best be understood as constituting a broader critique of the Enlightenment project, along the lines of Max Horkheimer and Theodor Adorno's *Dialectic of Enlightenment* (1944). In common with these authors, Foucault suggests that the neutral voice of scientific reason, that promised to liberate us from the tyranny of religious domination and superstitious fear, has itself become an instrument of control and normalisation. Moreover, Foucault makes the original and important criticism that the technologies of oppression and normalisation visible in the history of madness are insidiously pervasive in society more broadly. What appear to be local and exceptional instances of societal control actually reveal the workings of Enlightenment reason as it is made manifest more generally in institutional practice. The model of power with which Foucault is concerned, at this early stage in his thought, is the 'juridical' or negative form, which operates via repression, exclusion and stigmatisation, rather than the productive model of power that he will develop in the later genealogical works. In later decades, in fact, Foucault would return to the problem of the Enlightenment and call into question his own earlier suggestion that madness may offer a viable *alternative* to reason. In 'What is Enlightenment?' (1984), Foucault states that the Enlightenment perspective is too close to us historically and culturally to be actively 'chosen' or 'rejected'. It is already the framework in which we live and think, and the notion of its 'rejection' is therefore an impossibility. Moreover, engaging in the sophistry of acceptance or rejection involves adopting precisely the kind of dialectic reasoning of which Foucault is suspicious:

> [O]ne must reject everything that might present itself in the form of a simplistic and authoritarian alternative: you either accept the Enlightenment and remain within the tradition of its rationalism (this is considered a positive term by some and used by others, on the contrary, as a reproach), or else you criticize the Enlightenment and try to escape from its principles of rationality (which may be seen once again as good or bad).
>
> (*EW i*, p. 313)

We should instead approach the effects of Enlightenment thinking analytically via 'a series of historical inquiries that are as precise as possible' (*EW i*, p. 313). In this more sober response to the influence of the Enlightenment there is no longer the idea that it is an oppressive structure that the deviant voice of madness might somehow shatter; rather it is the dominant framework of thinking whose most pernicious qualities can best be tackled by careful analysis to establish where it may yield up discursive points of resistance to its own totalising capacity.

Foucault's *History of Madness* is an elaborate project which makes ambitious claims for the potency of madness in challenging the mainstream voice of reason (claims which, as we have seen, Foucault would later modify). However unusual and original this work may seem, however, it is important to view it in the context of its time as a contribution to a growing tendency to question both the treatment of the insane and the history of psychiatric medicine. For one thing, it was contemporaneous with the anti-medicine movement broadly, and the anti-psychiatry movement, associated with R. D. Laing, in particular (though Laing himself disowned this label).[7] Laing argued, like Foucault, that madness struggled to express something inadmissible in society, and that far from viewing them in terms of pathology, so-called psychotic episodes should be viewed as transformative and cathartic acts of articulation of all those emotions and impulses discouraged and disapproved of by society. In his earlier *Maladie mentale et psychologie* (1966), Foucault had critiqued very strongly the tendency of psychiatric diagnostic categorisation to efface the specificity of individual experience, subsuming idiosyncratic differences and revelations under tidy generalisations. Foucault's argument there and in the *History of Madness* – that apparently humane techniques of care and cure are in fact regimes of control – was a highly political, highly resonant one, which brought Foucault support from the anti-psychiatrists, but also attracted a good deal of negative criticism from 'humanist' psychiatric and psychologist thinkers and practitioners as well as mainstream historians, who challenged the validity of the broad-brush-stroke method of his archaeology and the accuracy of his description of a neat severing between the pre-modern and the modern approaches to folly.

One of the strongest critiques of Foucault's historical method is offered in Erik Midelfort's article, 'Madness and Civilization in Early Modern Europe'.[8] Midelfort refutes Foucault's ascription of freedom and acceptance to the mad during the Renaissance by demonstrating that the practice of confinement, which Foucault claims was an invention of the classical age, was in fact widespread before the seventeenth century. He also argues that the image of the Ship of Fools was no more than that: a symbolic representational image, which bore little resemblance to any social reality governing the *treatment* of the mad. Midelfort also argues, as does Roy Porter, that Foucault's heavy reliance on French sources elides the specificity of the establishment of the mental health profession in different European contexts. An extension of this criticism (indeed, one which can be levelled at all of Foucault's work) is its Eurocentric bias.[9] Still other critics, such as Jürgen Habermas and Gillian Rose, have argued that Foucault's approach to the Enlightenment in *Madness and Civilisation* is unacceptably one-sided, privileging a nihilistic denial of the considerable freedoms and rights that have been attained in recent history in the interests of promoting Foucault's resolutely anti-dialectical position.[10]

Defenders of Foucault's *History* include, most prominently, Colin Gordon, who has correctly pointed out that most of these critiques come from Anglo-American critics who have read the work only in the abridged English translated version, *Madness and Civilisation*. Gordon is able both to mitigate the accusation of sloppy history by returning to the – much longer – original French text of *Folie et déraison*, and to point to specific passages in the French that acknowledge a more balanced view of the Enlightenment.

However, the larger question that vexed historians was that of Foucault's historical methodology itself. To cite Lois McNay on this point, Foucault's history 'presents a challenge to conventional historiography by showing how the reconstruction of the past has been too often complicit in the structures of rationality that have marginalised and excluded the mad'.[11] A conventional empirical historian could have little sympathy with the empathic phenomenological history of marginality proposed here and – in differing ways and to differing degrees – throughout Foucault's corpus. On the other hand, revisionist historians and new historiographers in subsequent decades would be inspired by Foucault's tracing of histories (archaeologies/genealogies) of silenced voices, the writing of the small narratives that have gone unheard in the traditional 'grand narrative' of modern history. Andrew Scull, in a largely critical article on the *History*, argues that it is as a piece of avant-garde literature, of the sort produced, perhaps, by the 'mad' authors Foucault favours, rather than as a scholarly document, that this work is valuable. It is, he claims 'a provocative and dazzlingly written prose poem, but one resting on the shakiest of scholarly foundations and riddled with errors of fact and interpretation'.[12]

Foucault's *History* also attracted attention from his peers in the rarefied sphere of French philosophy. In 1963, Jacques Derrida delivered a public lecture on 'The Cogito and the History of Madness'.[13] Nominally acknowledging his debt to Foucault's work on mental illness, Derrida never the less went on to accuse Foucault of repeating in his book the very act of ethical violence that Foucault claims is perpetrated against madness: that of silencing its voice. As absolute alterity, Derrida argues, madness cannot be historicised, articulated or spoken for within the language of reason and logic. In writing a history of madness, Foucault is himself adopting the voice of reason that silences the absolute other. Derrida thus accuses Foucault of producing a work of structuralist totalitarianism that violates the integrity of the mad every bit as aggressively as psychiatry does in Foucault's account. Derrida claims that 'the misfortune of the mad, the interminable misfortune of their silence, is that their best spokesmen are those who betray them best; which is to say that when one attempts to convey their silence itself, one has already passed over to the side of the enemy, the side of order'.[14]

Derrida also disputes Foucault's understanding of Descartes's meditation on doubt. Foucault had argued that the philosophical importance of unreason lies in the function and qualities Descartes attributes to it in his meditation on doubt (the First Meditation). What, asks that philosopher of the *cogito*, can lead him to believe that he might have reason to doubt? First, his senses might be deceptive; secondly, he might be dreaming; thirdly, he might be being deceived by a malevolent force. There is one possibility, however, which Descartes is not willing to countenance: that he might be mad. He would, he concludes, have to be deluded to think himself like the delusional. Foucault's reading of this meditation is that, for Descartes, reason recognises itself as such by defining itself in contradistinction to what it is not: unreason. It is this act of recognition which precludes the possibility of madness. Derrida argues that Foucault is wrong to assume madness has a special status within this argument. All thought, he claims, is predicated on the exclusion of some element, some principle of negativity (a key tenet of Derrida's deconstructive method); therefore Cartesian thought does not merit being singled out here, and its reason/unreason binarism is not neatly mappable on to a political reading of the historical institutionalisation of techniques for excluding madness.

Foucault responded to Derrida in 1972 in a work that has been translated as the essay 'My Body, This Paper, This Fire' (*EW ii*, pp. 393–417). Adopting the strategy that his own defender Colin Gordon will later take up, Foucault argues that Derrida's reading of Descartes is flawed, as it relies on an inaccurate translation – here a modern French translation of Descartes's Latin original. Employing the impressive close reading method at which he is – when he chooses to be – so adept, Foucault dismisses several of Derrida's criticisms. He argues more broadly that Derrida's insistence that the exclusion of the negative is a technique of all systems of thought, and not exclusive to the case of Descartes and madness, points to a wilful ahistoricism in the deconstructionist's method and a resistance to understanding the functioning of specific discursive practices as nexuses of power relations and their exercise. Derrida, claims Foucault famously, substitutes for the specific political valency of 'discursive practices' mere 'textual traces' (*EW ii*, p. 416) and thereby establishes a 'pedagogy that teaches the pupil there is nothing outside the text' (*EW ii*, p. 416). The fundamental incompatibility of the two thinkers' projects does not prevent their dialogue about madness being a fruitful one, in which the imaginative strengths of Foucault's *Gedankenexperiment*, as well as its logical problems and shortcomings, are articulated for the reader.

The Birth of the Clinic

Foucault's other major work on the development of the health disciplines, *The Birth of the Clinic*, first published in 1963 in a collection edited for Gallimard by Canguilhem, offers a more localised example of the ways in which modern medicine developed than does *Madness and Civilisation*. A less boisterous and obviously polemical account than the earlier work, it focuses precisely on the social repercussions of the development of medical models and discourses between the end of the eighteenth and the middle of the nineteenth centuries – the period which witnessed a move from a 'medicine of species' to 'clinic-based' medicine. Foucault's close readings of medical treatises are interesting and offer valuable models for a discourse-sensitive analysis of texts. Indeed, regarding his political intentions, Foucault writes:

> I should like to make it plain once and for all that this book has not been written in favour of one kind of medicine as against another kind of medicine, or against medicine and in favour of an absence of medicine. It is a structural study [unusual choice of terminology for Foucault] that sets out to disentangle the conditions of its history from the density of discourse, as do others of my works.
>
> (*BC*, p. xxii)

As is often the case in Foucault's texts, despite such disclaimers, a consideration of power – which shades into an ethical comment on power – does emerge in this work. However, what Foucault is insisting upon here is that, unlike the *History of Madness* which, while nominally concerned with historical trends, also dallied ambivalently with a phenomenological theory of 'pure' madness pre-existing its subjection to discourse, *The Birth of the Clinic* will wed itself thoroughly to the historical method described as 'archaeology', which Foucault would go on to expound at length in *The Order of Things* and *The Archaeology of Knowledge* (see Chapter 3). 'Archaeology', in this sense, is a history unconcerned with individual experience or human agency: an inquiry which uncovers the system of rules underlying 'statements' (authorised utterances). The historical archaeology of medicine, then, sheds light on the silent rules producing the discourses that authorise themselves to pronounce on health and sickness in a given historical period. It identifies the conditions that were necessary for the emergence of the institutions and professions of clinic-based medicine in modernity. Notwithstanding the abandonment of any phenomenologically inflected model, however, *The Birth of the Clinic* is also concerned with thinking the condition of difference or alterity subjugated by processes of scientific authority and Enlightenment reason.

Foucault argues that in less than half a century, the way in which disease was conceptualised shifted radically. The classical concept of disease was as an entity that existed independently of its physical manifestation in particular anatomical symptoms, in a particular individual's body; the modern model – the one with which we are familiar still today – relies on the examination of a given body to reveal the nature and severity of the relevant disease activity. In positing this, Foucault introduces the idea that medicine shifted its focus from a 'language of fantasy' to a process of scrutiny, of 'constant visibility'. *The Birth of the Clinic* is noteworthy, then, for being the first work in which Foucault explains the importance of visuality and the scopic in regimes of power and knowledge. He opens the work with the following, striking words: 'This book is about space, about language, and about death; it is about the act of seeing, the gaze' (*BC*, p. ix). The book focuses on the moment when the medical gaze first comes into being, when doctors stop asking 'what is wrong' and begin to ask 'where does it hurt?'; when the patient steps up and takes centre stage under the spotlight of the doctor's scrutiny. The new medical gaze partitions the body into its components and essays an anatomy of disease. Foucault argues that the new model focuses on chronology – on the progression of a given disease as it is symptomatised in different parts of the body – rather than on the structural model that had established the 'species' of illness by means of analogy (so catarrh was to the throat as dysentery was to the intestines, etc.).

Foucault's historical reconceptualisation of anatomical medicine is as 'political', in the broadest sense, as was his revisionist history of the mental health disciplines. Where a standard history of medicine would describe the changes Foucault notes in terms of a narrative of progress, improved medical understanding, and increasing scientific sophistication, Foucault designates the shift as a 'syntactical reorganization of disease in which the visible and the invisible follow a new pattern' (*BC*, p. 195). As we would expect of Foucault, this reorganization is intimately involved with questions of power relations. The doctor's gaze 'is not faithful to truth, nor subject to it, without asserting, at the same time, a supreme mastery: the gaze that sees is a gaze that dominates' (*BC*, p. 39).

Where once, in classical medicine, the individual patient was irrelevant and the disease could be discussed and studied as a separate entity, suddenly, in clinical medicine, the patient became the central focus of the diagnostic process. Rather than seeing disease in terms of 'a pathological garden where God distributed species' (*BC*, p. 39), medics looked to the individual body to find the source of the ill. Foucault maps the 'pattern' of disease along vertical and horizontal axes. The classical model of disease was flat, horizontal, an immediately accessible truth, whereas the modern anatomical model, in which symptoms must be read on the body and interpreted to reveal the *underlying* disease, describes a vertical line of examination, a truth to be revealed by what we might call a medical archaeology.

This new focus on a deep-lying meaning that can be revealed by a skilled deciphering of somatic symptoms is traced to the popularity anatomical dissection which, Foucault noted, encouraged doctors to understand the effects of the disease on a living patient by examining the corpse of a person who had died from the illness: 'paradoxically, the presence of the corpse enables us to perceive it living' (*BC*, p. 183). Thus, the exploration of the body that is the medical right in modernity extends from the gaze to the touch, from surface observation to autopsy, revealing the hidden secrets of the inner anatomy for the doctor's edification. However, Foucault acknowledges that Marie François Xavier Bichat (1771–1802), on whose work he focuses, was not the first doctor to practice anatomical pathology. As early as the middle of the eighteenth century in Italy, Giovanni Battista Morgagni (1682–1771), commonly hailed as the father of anatomical pathology, was dissecting bodies. The meaning of the difference between these moments lies, Foucault argues, in the specificity of the 'anatomo-clinical' method. 'Bichat's eye is a clinician's eye, because he gives an absolute epistemological privilege to the *surface gaze*' (*BC*, p. 158). The clinical conception of anatomical pathology brought, Foucault argues, a new relationship with and conception of death. Where once death was 'the night into which disease disappeared', the point beyond which disease was no longer either accessible or relevant, suddenly it became the entry point into an understanding of the disease process. Between disease and life, death became the point of access to understanding and possessing the secrets of the body. The mastery aspired to in medicine culminated with a project of mastery over the secrets of death. 'But Bichat did more than free medicine of the fear of death. He integrated that death into a technical and conceptual totality in which it assumed its specific characteristics and its fundamental value as experience' (*BC*, p. 179). This is one of the few examples of Foucault's persistent but fraught interest in the concept of experience that surfaces in the book. And it surfaces in a very specific way and for a particular purpose: to chart the construction of an experience of individuality, through the medical realm, via language and death. In the differentiation of disease as morbidity, death in the 'anato-clinical' model (as opposed to death in Morgagni's anatomical pathology) gave the human subject individual truth: 'Death left its old tragic heaven and became the lyrical core of man, his invisible truth, his visible secret' (*BC*, p. 211). The effects of changes in medical models take on profoundly philosophical qualities in the closing pages of Foucault's book. What, he seems to be asking, if the discrete individual, the subject of the cogito were in fact the effect of the construction of the body and the individual patient that came into being through the scopic modalities of modern medicine? As Foucault points out, when the human being can take himself as the both subject and object of science, a new relationship with identity is created (an idea he would go on to pursue with regard to the human or social sciences in *The Order of Things*).

As in the case of Foucault's *History of Madness*, *The Birth of the Clinic* is an unapologetically Francocentric history. However, as a starting point – a discussion document, as Foucault intended it to be, for finding 'a method [to apply] in the confused, under-structured and ill-structured domain of the history of ideas' (*BC*, p. 241) – it is successful and has had considerable influence. European historians of medicine, such as Laurent Mucchielli, a scholar of medical and criminological history, have noted that the shift Foucault describes from abstract description of disease to detailed scrutiny of the body paved the way for a broad trend throughout the nineteenth century which involves increased concentration on corporeality, both living and dead, as capable of revealing truths of health and pathology. This includes the controversial science of phrenology, widespread in France in the 1830s, in which a person's moral character was felt to be legible from the shape of his head, and the anthropometry central to Cesare Lombroso's criminological science towards the end of the nineteenth century in Italy, in which inborn criminal traits could be read via a typology of jaws, noses, eyebrows and hands.[15] Forms of medical 'knowledge' such as these brought increased attention to bear on the intimate causal connections between biology and behaviour and made the body an object for further scrutiny and dissection.

The Birth of the Clinic is undoubtedly a significant study which helps us to rethink a history that appears – even more so than that of psychiatry – as a straightforward teleology of progress. The commonplace that the individual patient has always been the object of medical study is upended here, as it is revealed that he or she is in fact the end point of a long history and the defining feature of modern, as opposed to pre-modern, medicine. 'The clinic' in Foucault's account emerges as a geometry and as a discursive practice: 'both a new "carving up" of things and the principle of their verbalization in a form which we have become accustomed to recognizing as the language of a "positive science"' (*BC*, p. xx).

In some – quite subtle – ways, reading *The Birth of the Clinic* gives one the experience of witnessing the reconstitution of the history of the medic–patient relationship; its rituals and its roles, from the perspective of the patient. Unlike in the *History of Madness*, which, as we have seen, explicitly hoped to restore the silenced voice of madness, Foucault never states in *The Birth of the Clinic* that to restore the patient's view point is his intention. Yet, the clinician's gaze – that which is taken for granted as a necessary and inevitable part of medicine – is effectively called to attention and problematised throughout the work, as a particular reconfiguration of knowledge and power. Scholars such as David Armstrong have argued convincingly along these lines, positing that Foucault's re-historicising of the medical present offers a more suggestive and wide-ranging critique of the implications of medical knowledge and the doctor–patient relationship than empirical sociological accounts of the hospital experience have achieved.[16]

Finally, the popular contemporary fashion for patient-centred therapy and treatment – the notion that if the individual patient is the focus of the treatment, then the ethics of medical practice are assured – is given a different slant through Foucault's argument that putting the individual patient right at the centre of treatment does not necessarily lessen the power relation between the doctor's gaze/touch and the medicalised body – indeed, it may bring it all the more sharply into focus. Or, more radically, it may even create it ex nihilo. It is a beautifully subtle feature of Foucault's argument that the dominant gaze of modern clinical medicine is not totalising or universalising, but individualising. Individuality, which humanists and neo-liberals take to be that which must be defended from oppression, becomes nothing more than the effect of the operation of power in Foucault's anti-humanist, but still humane, text.

Chapter 3

Works: the death of man

Experience has shown that the human sciences, in their development, led to
the disappearance of man rather than to his apotheosis.

Michel Foucault

Implementing and refining the critical-historical method termed 'archaeology',
developed in his work on medicine, Foucault turns in 1966 to a consideration
of the underlying intellectual conditions that produced the modern disciplines
known as the human sciences. Having studied the rupture 'that every society finds itself obliged to make' between reason and madness, Foucault now
claimed that he wished 'to write a history of order' (*EW ii*, p. 261), elsewhere
formulated as a 'history of resemblances' (*OT*, p. xxvi). This history of order
and resemblances came in two parts: *Les Mots et les choses* (*The Order of Things:
An Archaeology of the Human Sciences*), published in 1966, and *The Archaeology
of Knowledge*, published three years later.

In an interview about *The Order of Things*, Foucault defines his refined
archaeological method in the following terms:

> By 'archaeology', I would like to designate not exactly a discipline, but a
> domain of research, which would be the following: in a society, different
> bodies of learning, philosophical ideas, everyday opinions, but also
> institutions, commercial practices and police activities, mores – all refer
> to a certain implicit knowledge [*savoir*] special to this society. This
> knowledge is profoundly different from the bodies of learning [*des
> connaissances*] that one can find in scientific books, philosophical
> theories, and religious justifications, but it is what makes possible, at a
> given moment, the appearance of a theory, an opinion, a practice.
>
> (*EW ii*, p. 261)

Foucault begins from the observation that in order for something to be thought or institutionalised as knowledge (*connaissances*), certain conditions for that type of thought to be possible must already be in place at a more fundamental level (*savoir*). To put it another way, without the existence of the underlying 'conditions of possibility' a given system of thought or body of knowledge would be impossible. Our ability to conceptualise the world is radically limited by the pre-existing field of 'the thinkable' at any historical moment. It is in its historical implications that Foucault's use of the concept 'condition of possibility' differs from the Kantian use of this term. For Kant, in the *Critique of Pure Reason* (1781), these conditions describe universal human capabilities or potentialities that are accessible from the point within consciousness from which we are required to think. For Foucault, they are wholly culturally and historically specific: what is humanly possible in one epoch simply may not be in another. Our ability to think in a certain way – to reason, to question, to analyse – is not essential to us as intelligent beings, but contingent on our location in time and space. Where Kant distinguishes between *a priori* knowledge (that which we can 'just' know, logically, prior to experience) and that which is *a posteriori* – based on experiential evidence – Foucault sets out to show that the category described by Kant as *a priori* actually designates an invisible set of underlying rules that make systems of thought and discourse historically possible. The whole project of *The Order of Things* can be seen, then, as an attempt to rethink Kant's concerns in *The Critique of Pure Reason* through the lens of an unusual historical rather than purely philosophical perspective.

While linguistic structuralist thinkers would point out that, of course, the linguistic system of grammar curtails and delimits the way in which we may think, Foucault looks beyond these purely language-based considerations – the tyranny of the 'phoneme' so central to post-Saussurian linguistics – to consider the unconscious rules according to which order is made out of experience. He thereby identifies what he calls 'epistemes'. The charge that this is Foucault's most structuralist work may be in part due to its terminology. If the phoneme is the smallest unit of linguistic signification, the episteme may be thought of as a single unit of epistemological contingency. Epistemes are, then, specificities on which order may be predicated. They cause certain forms and structures of knowledge to emerge in a given cultural period and at a given moment.

Foucault's study of these epistemes focuses, like Nietzschean genealogy and Bachelard's epistemology, on discontinuities rather than linearity, by which we should understand that the historical succession of the epistemes identified is without logical inevitability. Indeed, the work seeks to prove that knowledge and reason do not 'progress', as is commonly thought, but occur as a result of unpredictable epistemic changes and ruptures. Similarly, archaeology is a history without human agency. By this I do not mean that Foucault wishes to deny in this work the ethical or political importance or responsibility of the individual subject of history, but rather that archaeology focuses on identifying the common historical context in, and by means of which, a generation of individuals is both permitted to think and limited in the types of thought they can produce. History is commonly written, like a novel, as a series of adventures undergone by a protagonist or group, what post-modern thinkers have termed 'grand narratives'. Foucault wishes to establish here a history that looks deeper than individual experience or consciousness, and that questions our assumption that we are uniquely aware of, or in control of, the decisions we make: rather than having at our disposal an infinite world of thinkable possibilities, we are limited by our own – invisible – epistemic moment and its contingent rules.

The Order of Things

The Order of Things opens with Foucault recounting his own amusement and wonder at a passage of Borges, which quotes from 'a certain Chinese encyclopaedia' in which it is written that:

> [A]nimals are divided into (a) belonging to the Emperor, (b) embalmed, (c) tame, (d) sucking pigs, (e) sirens, (f) fabulous, (g) stray dogs, (h) included in the present classification, (i) frenzied, (j) innumerable, (k) drawn with a very fine camelhair brush (l) *et cetera*, (m) having just broken the water pitcher, (n) that from a long way off look like flies.
>
> (*OT*, p. xvi)

If a system of taxonomy does not seem familiar to us, it appears to us as nonsensical. Mixed with the humour Foucault finds in the Borges reference, however, is an uneasiness produced by the suspicion of 'a worse kind of disorder than that of the incongruous' (*OT*, p. xix). This worse disorder would be 'the disorder in which fragments of a large number of possible orders glitter separately' (*OT*, p. xix). Suddenly, the idea that wholly other ways of ordering the world may potentially exist or have existed comes into focus for Foucault. The citation from the fictional Chinese encyclopaedia leads us to wonder by what certitude we feel able to say for sure that two greyhounds resemble each other more than a cat does a dog, even if the cat and the dog are both frenzied or have both just broken a water pitcher. Our system of 'commonsensical' classification suddenly appears in doubt, under erasure, thanks to our confrontation with another potential way of ordering the world that is incompatible with our own.

This reveals as a principle 'the stark impossibility of thinking *that*' (*OT*, p. xvi), by which Foucault means that we habitually wear epistemological blinkers, conditioned by the ordering of knowledge in our own, given, historical epoch and outside of which we cannot conceive otherwise. *The Order of Things* leads us to understand that the world suddenly looks very different once we realise that our system of knowledge is not a neutral and verifiable truth, but a status quo we have arrived at almost by chance.

In order to analyse and problematise knowledge systems, we have to understand how they function. Foucault shows that classification appears as both essential to all forms of thought and, in its content, fragilely founded on arbitrary connections:

> Order is, at one and the same time, that which is given in things as their inner law, the hidden network that determines the way they confront one another, and also that which has no existence except in the grid created by a glance, an examination, a language; and it is only in the blank spaces of this grid that order manifests itself as depth as though already there, waiting in silence for the moment of its expression.
>
> (*OT*, p. xxi)

Foucault posits that between a given system and the philosophical interpretations that *explain* the need for a principle of order, there exists a fundamental domain: the unconscious one in which what initially made the order hang together has become lost. This domain, in which the ghost of an initial logic of systematisation – once transparent, now effaced – exists, is the domain with which *The Order of Things* is concerned. Foucault asserts: 'Thus, in every culture, between the use of what one might call the ordering codes and reflections upon order itself, there is the pure experience of order and its modes of being' (*OT*, p. xxiii). This is not a history of ideas, then, but a history of the epistemic field that makes certain ideas possible at certain moments, not at others. This is a field generally subject to cultural amnesia, so we are able to think that certain ways of understanding the world *just are*, rather than having their own aetiology and guiding context.

As well as focusing on textual and verbal taxonomies, *The Order of Things* is concerned with the realm of the visual, since representation in all its forms is one of the processes whose silenced history is restored. Foucault's first analysis in the whole book is of Velázquez's painting *Las Meninas* (1656). He analyses the painting as complexifying the structures of looking at and within a work of art. The tableau depicts, at the most basic level, an artist painting a portrait of the king and queen in the company of their daughter, who has come to watch, along with an assortment of her handmaids (*las meninas*) and a dog. However, the picture's composition is nowhere near so straightforward as I have just made it sound. When we look at the picture, our position as looker is rendered multiple by the gaze of both the painter and the king and queen, who are visible in the mirror, and who initially appear to return our look. However, we might also be in the position *of* the king and queen, looking at the spectacle. Thirdly, the vision in the mirror may instead reflect the image on the canvas within the picture, which the painter is depicted as working on, and of which we can only see the back. As Foucault puts it:

> In appearance [. . .] we are looking at a picture in which the painter is in turn looking out at us. A mere confrontation, eyes catching one another's glance, direct looks superimposing themselves upon one another as they cross. And yet this slender line of reciprocal visibility embraces a whole complex network of uncertainties, exchanges and feints. The painter is turning his eyes towards us only in so far as we happen to occupy the same position as his subject.
>
> (*OT*, p. 5)

The alignment of our gaze with the position of the king and queen's gaze, and the presence of the mirror, mean that 'no gaze is stable, or rather, in the neutral furrow of the gaze piercing at a right angle through the canvas, subject and object, the spectator and the model, reverse their roles to infinity' (*OT*, p. 5). Thus, in numerous ways, subject–object relations and spatial relations become confused, and the meaning of the painting resides in the way it makes us think about the role of absence, presence and perspective in representation.

Foucault offers us this pictorial example in order to suggest that the tableau problematises the possibility of straightforward representation in an age – the 'classical age' – in which, he argues, linguistic description was thought to be transparent, with no gap between words and things, and paintings were thought to offer an unproblematic window on to the world. For Foucault, then, *Las Meninas* offers a prescient critique of the capacity of representation to confirm an objective order visually: 'representation, freed finally from the relation that was impeding it, can offer itself as representation in its pure form' (*OT*, p. 18). For Foucault the foundations of modernity are found in the rejection of this classical epistemology, where representation is the dominant mode. He uses the example of *Las Meninas* to open the book whose overall argument is that all periods of history operate according to underlying conditions of truth that govern their production of discourse, but that subtle sea changes and shifts characterise the discontinuous history of knowledge. This 'final freeing' of representation from its marriage to a sovereign subject of representation must not be read to describe *progress* – merely to bear witness to *change*.

The Order of Things then goes on to historicise epistemology in three main periods, and to show the differing relationship of understanding between things in the world and the language system in each period. It begins with the end of the Renaissance and beginning of the classical age, and examines the shifts that occurred between their epistemological systems. In the Renaissance, states Foucault, the world was understood according to a system of 'similitude' or affinities between its objects. Thus aconite was seen to correspond to the eyes because of its formation and appearance. The dark seeds embedded in white resemble the human eye, and, to take the logical affinity a step further, these seeds were thought able to cure diseases of the eye. In the system of Renaissance knowledge, Foucault contends, magic and science were not in opposition or contradiction to one another, but were seen to be complementary systems for deciphering the meanings inherent in the world of things. Language, like eyes and aconite, was not thought of as a symbolic or representational system; rather – as the original French title of Foucault's work suggests – words too were 'things'. Words, that is, were entities that bore the same capacity for affinities, attractions and correspondences as other objects and elements, such as aconite and eyes.

The break with the Renaissance system of thought comes with the classical age, in which, according to Foucault, a mathematical system of classification came to predominate as the means of organising knowledge. Vast taxonomies and anatomies were produced, which focused not on affinities and similarity but on variation, measurement and number. These he calls *mathesis* and *taxinomia*. 'The ordering of things by means of signs constitutes all empirical forms of knowledge based on identity and difference' (*OT*, p. 61). Where *Las Meninas* caused its viewer to flicker between the rules governing knowledge at that time and an epistemological system of questioning and rupture that was proper to a later epoch, so, conversely, figures may continue to behave as if the unconscious stratum of knowledge of a bygone era were still the norm. Foucault's example here is Cervantes's *Don Quixote* (1605). Don Quixote's travels take place in the classical age of *mathesis*, but he pursues a Renaissance quest for affinities, expecting everything in the world to correspond to the romances he has read. However, Cervantes's revelation that Don Quixote's quest is invalid, that writing can no longer be understood as 'the prose of the world', marks the decisive moment of severance between these knowledge systems.

In the Renaissance thought-system of *divinatio*, says Foucault, signs existed before interpretation, bearing their covert meaning, waiting for the affinities between them to be realised. In classical *mathesis*, on the other hand, 'it is within knowledge itself that the sign is to perform its signifying function; it is from knowledge that it will borrow its certainty or its probability' (*OT*, pp. 65–6). The most important property of classical signs, says Foucault, is that they function to mark a relation of representation between two terms in the world – the sign and the signified – and 'what connects them is a bond established, inside knowledge, between the *idea of one thing* and the *idea of another*' (*OT*, p. 70). In the sixteenth century, the relation had three terms: 'that which was marked, that which did the marking, and that which made it possible to see in the first the mark of the second; and this last element was, of course, resemblance' (*OT*, p. 70). In the classical age, then, language and sign systems gained the arbitrary quality by which modern theorists characterise them. However, the question for the classical reader was how accurately sign systems were able to represent the nature of the 'real' world. And so the belief in mimesis was born.

Between the classical age and the modern period came another break, asserts Foucault. The origins of modern thinking are located here in a rejection of the classical taxonomical method of *mathesis*. The nineteenth century critiqued and problematised eighteenth-century *classification*, in favour of a method of *interpretation*. And language was to some extent 'emancipated' from the task that classical age knowledge had imposed upon it of effecting a perfect and seamless representation of things in the world. Just as Cervantes straddles Renaissance and classical epistemologies, it is Foucault's privileged author of sex, the Marquis de Sade, who sits between the classical and the modern modes. On the one hand, Sade's work belongs to the genre of libertinage, in which the tireless recounting and enumerating of pleasures and bodily practices is as paramount as yielding to the erotic instinct itself. On the other hand, Sade's writing is in excess of libertine conventions, as the attempt to convey inordinate sexual frenzy in enumerative language has the effect of showing up language's limits: language employed to this end becomes tired, repetitive and impoverished. The inadequate fit between bodily experience and language is thus revealed. Foucault explains:

> Sade attains the end of classical discourse and thought. He holds sway precisely upon their frontier. After him, violence, life and death, desire and sexuality will extend, below that level of representation, an immense expanse of shade which we are now attempting to recover, as far as we can, in our discourse, in our freedom, in our thought.

> (*OT*, p. 229)

Just as in *The Birth of the Clinic*, which foregrounds an altered relationship with death as part of the specificity of the clinical method and modern imagination, so death haunts the closing sections of *The Order of Things* and characterises modern epistemology. And just as language is no longer seen as transparent or equal to the task of containment of meaning, so in the field of economic and political analysis (e.g. Marxian critique), attention is increasingly paid to the hidden, unrepresented concept of labour, something that is not visible at the surface level of the fiscal transaction or economic exchange. And in the natural sciences, 'what makes it possible to characterize a natural being is no longer the elements that we can analyse in the representations we make for ourselves of it and other beings, it is a certain relation within this being which we call its organic structure' (*OT*, p. 257). The epistemic focus turns, then, to 'the dark, concave, inner side' (*OT*, p. 258) of representation; a realm beyond visibility 'in a sort of behind-the-scenes world' (*OT*, p. 259).

The dissolution of the possibility of observing straightforward representation leads to a concern with the source and origin of representation itself. The subject of knowledge – sovereign 'man' (Foucault and his translators are not sensitive to gender-neutral language) – appears in a unique light in the modern age. As well as being the putative bearer of knowledge, he becomes that which is studied to find meaning. When the compilation and observation of descriptive systems give way to analysis (when objects are seen in terms of their *function* rather than merely their *position* within a given system), the conditions are in place for the disciplines of economics, linguistics and the life sciences to come into being. What is unique to the modern period, then, is that 'man' can take himself as both the subject and the object of his interrogations, as we have already seen in the case of development of medicine in *The Birth of the Clinic*.

And, as in that work, the inward-looking gaze upon which modern epistemology is founded leads to a human-centric and thereby death-bound consciousness, what Foucault calls 'the analytic of finitude'. In modernity, historicity begins to dominate analyses of economics, natural history and language; and history is that which limits human capacity (a good example of this would be Malthus's fear of overpopulation as bringing with it the threat of death). The dramatic outcome of Foucault's analyses in this work is his closing statement that 'man', the 'recent invention' (*OT*, p. 422) and object of study of the social sciences, is a historically contingent construct which, with the next epistemic shift, is liable to be 'erased, like a face drawn in sand at the edge of the sea' (*OT*, p. 422). Thus we return to where we started: with the observation that Foucault's archaeology, while using similar language to Kant's metaphysics, stands in opposition to an ahistorical Kantian humanism. For Foucault, the human subject as the modern social sciences create it is a mere truth effect of the operations of history, and can be plotted in a discontinuous map of the thinkable. Foucault is writing in the tradition of Heidegger and Nietzsche here, in assuming that the analytic of finitude on which the human sciences are founded describes the way in which 'Man' simply takes over the place of God, Power, Truth, Logos etc. as the core of thought in modernity.

The Order of Things: responses, critiques and intertexts

The strange and oft-commented-upon impression that one has while reading *The Order of Things* is that Foucault is writing a history that is topographical rather than chronological. The potential danger of Foucault's use of the concept of discontinuous epistemes is that they seem to hang in radical disjuncture from each other, with no sense at all of historical movement. This notion of a frozen history, or a history in thrall to death, is described several times by Foucault's commentators. For Allan Megill, 'to enter into *Les Mots et les choses* is to enter into a world whose fundamental metaphor is the metaphor of arrangement in space; it is to enter into a world that is strangely silent and unmoving, into a frozen world of penetrating glances and frozen gestures'.[1] Foucault attempts to convey the sense that epistemes work like a constellation of already long-dead stars that continue to glimmer after their death, shining the treacherous light of an outmoded knowledge on us. This is a deliberately anti-establishmentarian type of history, and a type of writing that affects a break with continuist historical projects and their focus on progress. For detractors of *The Order of Things*, however, of whom Jean-Paul Sartre was probably the most eminent, in essaying this, Foucault is guilty of 'replacing the cinema with the magic lantern',[2] that is, of pursuing a sterile and regressive line of inquiry; of undoing valuable work that has been done; of being in some ways an intellectual Luddite. (As a thinker so opposed to teleologies of progress, Foucault may well have chosen to interpret Sartre's slight as a compliment rather than a damning criticism.) Yet the sparseness and sterility of this work is more than just a philosophical and stylistic idiosyncrasy or sophistry. It has the very political aim, consistent with the intellectual climate of 1960s France, of trying to think a history of knowledge and power apart from the socio-economic factors privileged by Marxist theorists. By foregrounding the significance of the *a priori* episteme, Foucault attempted to avoid a reductive reading of power and knowledge in which given systems and institutions are isolated, prioritised or scapegoated, a critique he would later make of his early studies of the institutions of mental health and of medicine, where the epistemological domain of medicine had been too neatly conflated with repression, even though there was repression outside of medicine and the evidential texts of medicine didn't always conform to repressive institutional forms.[3]

Moreover, the guiding premiss of *The Order of Things* – the idea that the rules by which we structure meaning, impose order and separate the normal from the abnormal are not inevitable, natural or – in any simple sense, 'true', but are wholly socially and historically constructed according to unconscious sets of governing rules – is not unique to Foucault but is also expressed in slightly different terms in contemporaneous Anglo-American texts in the field of sociology. In 1966, the same year as *Les Mots et les choses* appeared in France, Peter L. Berger and Thomas Luckman published in the USA *The Social Construction of Reality*. This is one of the first studies to question the philosophical status of 'what passes for "knowledge"',[4] and to critique 'objectivation, institutionalization and legitimation [as] directly applicable to the problems of the sociology of language, the theory of social actions and institutions, and the sociology of religion'.[5] Although the two projects do not have identical aims – Berger and Luckman's work is not concerned to the same extent as Foucault's with an anti-humanist agenda – the arrival of these works in the same year announces a moment of rupture from the commonplace that 'knowledge' is constituted by a set of unquestionable and objective bases of truth that progressively gain in accuracy, thanks to the advances of progress. In this, Foucault's *The Order of Things* is making a particularly French, post-structuralist contribution to a broader intellectual project of questioning the inevitable status of forms of knowledge and social organisation.

As we have seen with Foucault's writing on madness, *The Order of Things* also attracted criticisms that focused on the historical validity of Foucault's assertions regarding the periods he describes and the epistemological breaks between them that he charts. Some of these seek to discredit certain aspects of Foucault's long history – such as George Huppert's argument that the account presented of the Renaissance, in which magic and science co-existed harmoniously and in a complementary fashion, is erroneous. Huppert corrects Foucault by showing that scientific and humanist thinking in the sixteenth century was, in fact, highly critical of magic.[6] G. S. Rousseau asserts, in a more forceful gesture of rejection of the historiographical method as a whole, that in *The Order of Things* 'chronological labels actually play no part in Foucault's analysis and it is therefore a waste of time to examine them seriously'.[7] Lemert and Gillan have argued that 'episteme' was not a particularly useful concept, as it suggested closed-off systems, unconnected by a trajectory of time. They judge that Foucault would have laid himself open to fewer charges of failing to produce a history, and producing instead a work of structuralism, if he had not employed the term.[8]

More violent criticisms than these slights on its historical method have also been levelled at Foucault's 'book about signs'. As Gilles Deleuze summarises, 'certain malevolent people say that [Foucault] is the new representative of a structural technology or technocracy. Others, mistaking their insults for wit, claim that he is a supporter of Hitler, or at least that he offends the rights of man (they will not forgive him for having proclaimed "the death of man")'.[9] One can argue that Foucault's next work, *The Archaeology of Knowledge*, is an attempt to show what he really meant by this gesture, and how a criticism of the sovereign subject of modernity is far from being an unethical or homicidal project; it is, in fact, a necessary one for redressing the fallacies of historical method and the arrogance of humanism.

The Archaeology of Knowledge

The Archaeology of Knowledge picks up on the anti-humanist note with which *The Order of Things* closes and attempts to refine the historical methods employed in that work. It also introduces numerous conceptual terms for describing the processes that Foucault is 'digging up', many of which do not resurface again in the rest of his work. This is an odd book in many ways, which marks both an attempt to clarify some of the methodological premises set out in *The Order of Things* and a foray into the workings of knowledge so abstract in kind that many commentators have found its style and method *de trop*. In the introduction to the work, Foucault states, in response to the criticisms of his previous book that I have outlined above, that 'in *The Order of Things*, the absence of methodological signposting may have given the impression that my analyses were being conducted in terms of cultural totality' (*AK*, p. 18). This was, he goes on, a danger 'intrinsic to the enterprise itself, since, in order to carry out its task, it had first to free itself from [. . .] various methods and forms of history' (*AK*, p. 18). The *Archaeology* retains the earlier work's project of examining the rules governing order, but supplements, and to some extent supplants, the concept of 'episteme' by that of 'the archive', to signify the general condition of possibility governing what can or cannot be thought at a given historical moment. If epistemes spelt out the conditions necessary for a proposition to signify, then the 'archive' describes the way in which epistemes cluster together to produce the fields of knowledge that apply in modernity, such as medicine, grammar or economics. Foucault also introduces a fuller concept of discourse than he has hitherto essayed, with the notions of the 'statement' (*l'énoncé*) the 'discursive function' and 'discursive formations'. The statement is a unit of discourse – an utterance – but one that takes place in a specific context, within a 'discursive formation'. To be a statement a sentence has to have an authorised place within a knowledge system. Unfortunately, Foucault provides few concrete examples in the book, so that the concept can seem rather abstract. It is also slightly confusing that *l'énoncé* is a term borrowed from the technical language of linguistics, but without retaining the same meaning, so that (like the proximity of 'episteme' to 'phoneme' and 'matheme' – the latter a Lacanian concept), Foucault's archaeology flirts unnecessarily closely with the currents of thought with which it wishes to avoid being associated.[10]

The Archaeology of Knowledge is, perhaps more than anything else, a rather fractured guidebook on how to do an archaeological reading. Foucault spells out a method of archaeological reading based on sensitivity to both the microcosm and the macrocosm of the relationship between the statement and the discursive formation. Statements can be recognised as such by observation of the discursive formation to which they belong. Yet, simultaneously, the status of a discursive formation can be ascertained only by an analysis of the individual statements that constitute it and are governed by it. This principle by which one discursive formation can be distinguished from another is termed a 'system of dispersion'. It is governed by four sets of 'rules of formation': objects, enunciative modalities, strategies and concepts.

If the previous 'archaeologies' have been histories deliberately devoid of ontology and individual agency, the *Archaeology of Knowledge* takes this a step further, as can be gleaned from an examination of what Foucault means when he talks of 'enunciative modalities'. The individual does not possess discourse or make discursive meaning. Rather, discursive formations create subject positions that can – and must – be occupied by speaking individuals, such as that of the doctor who is authorised to diagnose your ailment, while I, as a cultural theorist, am not. 'This status of the doctor', says Foucault, 'is generally a rather special one in all forms of society and civilization. He is hardly ever an undifferentiated or interchangeable person. Medical statements cannot come from anybody' (*AK*, p. 56). Secondly, the discourse of the doctor acquires further legitimacy in issuing from an appropriate location or 'institutional site', such as a clinic, consulting room or hospital. And each of these three exemplary sites has a different internal structure proper to it as well as fitting differently within the network of social institutions of which it is a part. (For example, as Foucault points out, hospitals contain 'a differentiated and hierarchized medical staff' [*AK*, p. 56–7].) Thirdly and finally, the enunciative modality comprises the position the subject occupies with regard to the specific field of knowledge – he or she may be a listening subject, questioning subject, or seeing subject within a given situation, with each role carefully delineated and delimited by and within a given discursive context. The three elements of the enunciative modality reveal that 'discourse is not the majestically unfolding manifestation of a thinking, knowing, speaking subject, but, on the contrary, a totality in which a network of distinct sites is deployed' (*AK*, p. 60).

Foucault defines himself at this moment as a 'happy positivist' – somewhat ironically, perhaps, given his critique elsewhere of the scientific and rationalistic currents of thought to which the label 'positivism' is usually applied (another example of Foucault's tendency to use language – and particularly technical terms – in a deliberately perverse and idiosyncratic way). By 'positivist', however, Foucault simply means that he is concerned with observing the conditions of the possibility of historical discourse without any recourse to the complicating factors of human personality or intention. He is, as we have seen, attempting to rewrite of 'a history of discourses which, until now, has been animated by the reassuring metaphors of life or the intentional continuity of the lived' (*AK*, p. 231). Foucault's method at this moment of his writing is also a method of positivity in the sense that he does not, as his essay on 'Nietzsche, Freud, Marx' has shown, have any time for the notion of 'depth claims' in thought, or deep hidden meanings that can be discovered in history via the 'correct' interpretation of sources. As Lemert and Gillan put it: '[Foucault's] historical method emphasises the reconstruction of the positivity of rules operating in history on concrete social practices. Since rules, in his sense, are not givens, they must be reconstituted by the historian.'[11] The book is largely an experiment in testing the limits to which a non-humanist historiography can be pushed.

Critiques of Foucault's archaeological theory of discourse have focused on his problematic insistence that discourse can be understood as a largely abstract practice, 'governed by analysable rules and transformations' (*AK*, p. 232), as this fails to account for the socio-political and institutional workings of specific discursive organisations. This is a criticism levelled particularly forcefully by Hubert Dreyfus and Paul Rabinow.[12] In his inaugural lecture 'The Order of Discourse' in 1970, Foucault would go on to address this lacuna, by introducing a distinction between the 'truth value' of a proposition – which archaeology cannot determine – and its 'acceptability', that is, its belonging in both a discursive and non-discursive context, e.g. a disciplinary practice located in a historical and political sphere. Statements are therefore understood as true because they meet conditions of acceptability, not because they are 'in truth'.

Ernesto Laclau and Chantal Mouffe raise a different objection from that made by Dreyfus and Rabinow regarding Foucault's method. It centres on the distinction, insisted upon in 'The Order of Discourse', between discursivity and the nondiscursive. In short, they argue that if the object becomes an object of discourse only in so far as it acquires meaning within the conditions of its discursive formation, the concept of non-discursivity is redundant. Non-discursivity is more properly pre-discursivity: a condition of being prior-to-becoming discourse. However, this would be a condition internal to, not in tension with, discourse itself. Foucault's insistence on a distinction between these terms weakens his theory for Laclau and Mouffe, because it undermines his broader stated project of thinking history outside of dualisms and binaries which tend to shade into dialectics.[13]

It is possible to speculate that before Foucault reached a stage in his conceptualisation of 'discourse' in which that privileged term of his opus was capable of bearing its full political weight – a stage that would lead from the archaeological method to the genealogical one and embroil him in a consideration of the operations of power and knowledge – he needed first to void it entirely of human intentionality and 'personal' meaning. This message is given in the striking closing words of the conclusion of the *Archaeology*, a conclusion which takes the form of an imaginary dialogue between Foucault and one of his detractors. The final sentences, which both echo and modify the closing words of *The Order of Things*, announce the foolishness of failing to realise the non-individuality of discourse, its function as impersonal system:

> Discourse is not life: its time is not your time; in it, you will not be reconciled to death; you may have killed God beneath the weight of all that you have said; but don't imagine that, with all that you are saying, you will make a man that will live longer than he.
>
> (*AK*, p. 232)

This is a grim warning against the arrogance of the fantasy that, having 'killed God', humanity can now reign supreme as the limit-point of knowledge, consciousness and meaning. That Foucault returns again to this point persuades me that the emptying out of referential content in *The Archaeology of Knowledge*, a feature that has irritated so many readers, is not in the service of a dry structuralism, but is a heavy-handed but insistent rhetorical strategy for showing that the alternative to theocracy need not be a complacent humanism.

This brings us to the end of our reading of the works produced at the height of Foucault's archaeological 'period', and it is fitting that we close with a reference to a Nietzschean idea, since Nietzsche's methodology would colour so prominently the genealogy Foucault would go on to develop. Perhaps the most surprising thing about Foucault's work in the archaeological vein is the popularity of *The Order of Things*. *Les Mots et les choses*, a difficult work by anyone's standards, actually became a best-seller in France, although presumably, as David Macey has commented, 'many more copies were bought than were read'.[14] Published in the same year as Lacan's *Ecrits* and Barthes's *Critique et vérité*, it appeared when French critical theory – and particularly the 'structuralist turn' – was in its heyday and carried an irresistible *cachet*. (Foucault's sales figures no doubt benefited from the popular perception – Foucault would have said misperception – that his work in this vein was a structuralist manifesto.) *The Archaeology of Knowledge*, a more arid and less rhetorically dazzling text, did not attract the same popularity. It remains rather a book for specialists, expanding and refining some of the points Foucault introduced in

The Order of Things; redressing some criticisms, while inviting a whole series of fresh ones; pursuing a history without human agency; and placing centre stage for the first time the concept of discourse that would undergo massive transformations throughout the course of his work.

Works: authors and texts

We write to become other than what we are.

Michel Foucault

While most British and American university programmes in Literary Theory and Modern Critical Theory include works by Foucault on their bibliographies (most commonly the essay 'What is an Author?', 1969), his place in literary studies is not unproblematic. Neither Terry Eagleton's classic *Literary Theory: An Introduction*[1] nor Jefferson and Robey's *Modern Literary Theory: A Comparative Introduction*[2] – books produced during the mid-1980s, the hey day of the Anglo-American trend for critical theory – accord more than a passing mention to Foucault under the rubric of post-structuralism. This may be accounted for by the fact that it is simply not easy to 'do' a Foucaldian reading of a piece of literature or other cultural product in the way that one can 'do' a psychoanalytic, Marxist or phenomenological reading. This is because, rather than putting forward a theory of literature that one can 'apply' in a straightforward sense, Foucault's thought is concerned, first, with analysing the necessary conditions that allow literary values to be thought or discursively expressed at given moments, and, secondly, with observing the evacuation from literary language of individual authorial identity and systems of transparent meaning, in order to give access to 'the lightning-flash' (*MC*, p. 264) in which the otherwise silenced voices of madness or transgression can speak. It is literary writing for Foucault that renovates the way in which we think, and challenges assumptions about a subject of reason, a sovereign identity. In this, then, Foucault's task with regard to literature has strong similarities to the concerns he has brought to bear on the history of madness and the archaeology of knowledge discussed in previous chapters. In what follows, I shall demonstrate the character of Foucault's writing on writing.

History and aesthetics

We have seen that in *The Order of Things*, Foucault used literature – namely the writings of Sade – to exemplify the historical dissolution of the classical belief in the possibility of perfect mimetic representation that characterises modernity and post-modernity. Sade *announces* the modern age. Language is pushed to its representational limits in the modern age and becomes self-referential. Modern language has 'nothing to do but shine in the brightness of its being' (*OT*, p. 327). As language starts to deform and break free, not only of mimetic function but of the rules of grammar and – in the case of poetry – of prosody, challenging the expected link between form and content, so a new aesthetic and ontological model emerges. The French poets of modernity, particularly the Symbolist Stéphane Mallarmé, are important here as they exemplify for Foucault a revelation about literature and the identity of the authorial voice. If Nietzsche shows us the importance of always asking of a text 'who is speaking?', then, in modernity, the 'Mallarméan discovery of the word in its impotent power' is able to answer the question. Language itself, says Foucault, is speaking, with 'no other law than that of affirming – in opposition to all other forms of discourse – its own precipitous existence' (*OT*, p. 327). The subject – and object – of *avant garde* literature is language: its ambition, its inadequacy, its ultimate impotence. In this assertion of the primacy of language, Foucault's project may appear to be very close to that of the most strident structuralists, Barthes, in those works dating from the period of his concern with 'high structuralism',[3] or Roman Jakobson who, in his collaborative article with Claude Lévi-Strauss, so effectively and devastatingly stripped Baudelaire's poem 'Les Chats' (The Cats) of any sensuous or affective referentiality and showed instead how a poem is a closed system whose meaning relies on the tight arrangement of grammar, rhyme and syntax.[4] However, Foucault's concern is not solely with the rules governing language (surprisingly, perhaps, given that this was the guiding method of the archaeology essayed in *The Order of Things*). It is Foucault's enduring fascination with the marginal, exceptional, irrational – and our apprehension of it in a given historical time and space – so prominently visible in *The History of Madness* that makes his treatment of literature different from that of an early Barthes or a Jakobson.

In Foucault's essay on Georges Bataille, 'A Preface to Transgression' (1963), a concern for the rules produced by historical contingency is wedded intimately to the question of the significance of the concept of 'transgression' for that writer. Bataille argues in *Eroticism* (1957) that human beings are isolated, bounded, separate beings inhabiting a world of discontinuity. It is only in 'limit experiences' – namely, for Bataille, eroticism and death – that our boundaries dissolve temporarily and we achieve a state of continuity. Eroticism is distinct from mere sex, as the former is the sexual impulse expressed in the social rather than the animal realm. The social world structures our behaviour within the limits of taboos and prohibitions, erecting codes and rules governing what is permissible and tempering the violence and selfishness of human beings. Eroticism is the experiential zone within which taboos are transgressed. Sex and death are intimately related in eroticism because eroticism is 'assenting to life up to the point of death'.[5] Or, as Bataille puts it in *The Accursed Share*: 'Anguish, which lays us open to annihilation and death, is always linked to eroticism; our sexual activity finally rivets us to the distressing image of death, and the knowledge of death deepens the abyss of eroticism.'[6] The use of the term 'anguish' is not superfluous here; in Bataille's system eroticism is a traumatic, shattering experience in which notions of the fixed self, the personality, are destroyed. It is perhaps this quality of Bataille's thought that made the author so important to Foucault. This idea of bodily pleasure as the means by which social identities are revealed as fictions will be a tenet of Foucault's final writings on sexuality. (See chapters 6 and 7.)

Culture formulates taboos and transgressions to protect the artificial, capitalist economy of production, functionality and work (discontinuity) from the abyssal pull of sex and violence (continuity). The principles of excess, waste and anti-utilitarianism are grouped under the umbrella of 'transgression'. However, transgression as such does not constitute an absolute rejection of the social or a total break from it. Rather, occasional outbursts of excess – crime, sexual perversion – draw attention to transgression as limit, show up its workings and thereby ultimately reassert the regimented boundaries of the social order. The relationship between taboo and transgression, therefore, is dialectical for Bataille: transgression acknowledges and completes the taboo.[7]

Bataille asserts that the most powerful form of erotic excess occurred in the context of the religious rituals of pre-Reformation Christianity. Unlike in purely secular modern eroticism, the proximity and mixing of the sacred and the profane allowed for an unparalleled intensity. Bataille's writing on erotic transgression is read by Foucault in the 'Preface to Transgression' as being predicated on a specific historical-cultural consciousness and as a comment on the philosophical and experiential condition within an atheistic world view:

> A rigorous language, as it arises from sexuality, will not reveal the secret of man's natural being, nor will it express the serenity of anthropological truths, but rather, it will say that he exists without God; the speech given to sexuality is contemporaneous, both in time and in structure, with that through which we announced to ourselves that God is dead.
>
> (*EW ii*, p. 70)

Foucault argues, then, that Bataille's quest to represent 'limit experience' through theoretical writing and through his pornography of excess (of which *The Story of the Eye*, 1928, is the most celebrated example) is a result of a post-Nietzschean consciousness, marked by an awareness of the death of God and of the modern human being's moral groundlessness. In a world without moral certainties, transgression has a particular quality: it 'is neither violence in a divided world (in an ethical world) nor a victory over limits (in a dialectical or revolutionary world) and, exactly for this reason, its role is to measure the excessive distance that it opens at the heart of the limit' (*EW ii*, p. 74). Foucault reads Bataille, then, deliberately against the grain of his dialectical debt, re-viewing him through a Nietzschean rather than a Hegelian lens. In this model, excess, with no relation to the divine, to an ultimate exteriority, pushes only against the limits of identity. However, for Foucault transgression is not a concept that can be recovered within dialectical reason; it 'is not related to the limit as black to white' (*EW ii*, p. 73). Although Foucaldian transgression acknowledges a limit, it does not exist in a relation *with* it, but is a singular experience which cannot be assimilated to reason (much as Foucault had wanted madness to be in the *History of Madness*). In this refusal of dialectical reasoning, Foucault's gesture comes surprisingly close to the ethical philosopher and Talmudic scholar Emmanuel Lévinas, who attempts in *Totality and Infinity* (1961) to think the ethical outside of a dialectical relationship of reason, by imagining the encounter between two separate entities irreducible to each other (infinity), rather than two beings relating within a subject–object structure (totality).[8] Foucault calls the recognition of limit outside of dialectics 'non-positive affirmation' or 'contestation' (*EW ii*, p. 74). This contestation would involve an interminable movement of questioning, a refusal of certainties, rather than the assertion of an alternative order.

If modern philosophy is caught for Foucault in unhelpful thrall to dialectical reasoning, Bataille's celebration of the power of the transgressive experience releases within the sphere of literature energies internal to language that force us as readers to the limits of consciousness and rationality: to realise that language and philosophy without a subject are not the end of philosophy but the birth of a new possibility of thought. What is perhaps most striking in this at once dense and dazzling essay is the way in which Foucault ties concepts of limitlessness and extremity, apparently paradoxically, to contingency and history: the limit experience may be felt as shattering and transcendental, but its expression is intimately dependent on historical modes of thinking. It could not have been conveyed in the form Bataille executes prior to a Nietzschean atheistic consciousness.

This idea is developed in Foucault's essay on Pierre Klossowski, 'The Prose of Actaeon' (1964), which asks what happens to signs in a world beyond God, taking as its starting point Nietzsche's famous question regarding how to respond to a demon who says to one:

> 'This life as you now live it and have lived it, you will have to live once more and innumerable times more . . . The eternal hourglass of existence is turned upside down again and again, and you with it, speck of dust!' Would you not throw yourself down and curse the demon who spoke thus? Or have you experienced a tremendous moment when you could reply to him: 'you are a god, and I have never heard anything more divine!'[9]

In contradistinction to wrestling with the knotty question of how to tell good from evil, Foucault asks 'but what if, on the contrary, the Devil, the Other, were the Same' (*EW ii*, p. 123). He then goes on to describe a textual world – Klossowski's – in which this reversal, transposition and doubling occur: in which gods and devils become each other.

'In Klossowski's work', writes Foucault, 'the reversal of situations occurs in a moment, with a switching of sides. [. . .] The good become wicked, the dead come back to life, rivals reveal themselves to be accomplices, executioners are subtle rescuers, encounters are prepared long in advance, the most banal phrases have a double meaning' (*EW ii*, p. 128). In the consciousness evoked in this textual world, we are in the realms not so much of the 'sign' as of the 'simulacrum'. Foucault is prescient in his use of this term. It is a term which would become central to the post-modern philosophy of Jean Baudrillard, who argues that there is no original preceding the series of copies; there are only copies of copies. For Foucault, simulacra are the markers of a historical and ontological paradox. They indicate how the Other might be the Same, as simulation and dissemblance order the world voided of a clear-cut moral distinction between gods and demons. The characters in Klossowski 'do not simulate anything; they simulate themselves' (*EW ii*, p. 129). Simulacra mark, as Simon During puts it, 'an absence across an unbridgeable distance, they double each other across a limit marked and broken by the death of a God who never existed, and whose (imaginary) existence forms a limit on whose far side the Other can always be a version of the Same'.[10] Foucault argues, rather implausibly but strikingly, that what we find in the post-Nietzschean consciousness of Klossowski is a 'rediscovery' of the kind of simulation under which Western culture has always operated since the ancient Greeks; a tendency broken or disavowed only by the doctrinal religious insistence on signs which 'Catholics scrutinize' (*EW ii*, p. 131) to find the truths of their souls. While this historical statement is sweeping, nevertheless Foucault's focus on the simulacrum in this essay crucially anchors it in history, not in an ahistorical (structuralist) synchronic realm.

Similarly, in the much later essay on the history of philosophy, 'What is Enlightenment?' (1984), after Kant's essay of the same name, Foucault asserts the historical specificity of aesthetic possibility. Here, Foucault asks what it is that constitutes specifically *modern* philosophy; how the condition of philosophy today differs from what it was in former times. Philosophy, like everything else, is located in time and space; and 'modern' philosophy operates according to post-eighteenth-century Enlightenment values of reason. However, in order to answer his question fully, Foucault shifts focus from Kant to Baudelaire, from ethics to aesthetics, and argues that a mode of critical questioning of the real, rather than an acceptance of dogma and doctrine, must constitute modern thought. The subject of modernity is not the scientific rationalist, but Baudelaire's dandified *flâneur*: 'Modern man, for Baudelaire, is not the man who goes off to discover himself, his secrets and his hidden truth; he is the man who tries to invent himself. This modernity does not "liberate man in his own being"; it compels him to face the task of producing himself' (*EW i*, p. 312). From the example of Baudelaire's reflection on the modern artist, mixing the contingent with the eternal to produce ever new effects, Foucault can reformulate Kant's project of Enlightenment questioning. Rather than it being a matter of knowing 'what limits knowledge [*connaissance*] must renounce exceeding, [. . .] the critical question today must be turned back into a positive one: in what is given to us as universal, necessary, obligatory, what place is occupied by whatever is singular, contingent, and the product of arbitrary constraints?' (*EW i*, p. 315). In the ethical as in the aesthetic realm, for Foucault the task of the thinker is to challenge epistemology that passes as neutral and universal in order to isolate its specificity in a historical moment and its politically interested context.

Language in a vacuum

In tandem with his continued concern to isolate the historic specificity of what may be thought and expressed, Foucault is equally interested in literature for its capacity to articulate the fallacy of the cogito, the essential emptiness of human identity. His essay on Maurice Blanchot, 'The Thought of the Outside', is concerned with that writer's evocation in words of extreme or limit experiences. In this, we see a link with Bataille, although the depersonalised asceticism that characterises Blanchot's writing for Foucault could not be more different in kind to Bataille's frenzied pornography. Both, however, are examples of 'a language from which the subject is excluded' (*EW ii*, p. 149).

For Foucault, Blanchot's texts succeed in epitomising the effacement of the author's stamp of personality, such that:

> So far has he withdrawn into the manifestation of his work, so completely is he, not hidden from his texts, but absent from their existence and absent by virtue of the marvellous force of their existence, that for us he is that thought itself – its real, absolutely distant, shimmering, invisible presence, its necessary destiny, its inevitable law, its calm, infinite, measured strength.
>
> (*EW ii*, p. 151)

The 'thought of the outside' referred to in the title announces the rejection of reflective models of writing that fall back on conscious interiority and attempt to represent experience in the mimetic mode of realist fiction. Instead, Blanchot's discourse, argues Foucault, consents to go to the edge of language and to *undo* rather than to create images 'until they burst and scatter in the lightness of the unimaginable' (*EW ii*, p. 153). Deleuze writes that 'Foucault echoes Blanchot in denouncing all linguistic personology and seeing the different positions for the speaking subject as located within a deep anonymous murmur without beginning or end.'[11] These essays on literary practice, then, constitute illustrative arguments in rejection of the philosophy of consciousness and celebrate a truth that does not lie in reason.

The relationship between language and the void at the limits of rationality may be said to be the fundamental source of Foucault's interest in *avant garde* literature. For Foucault, madness and creative transgression are linked by their liminality and marginality. In 1964, Foucault wrote of 'the general form of transgression of which madness has, for centuries been the visible face' (*EW ii*, p. xvii); in *Madness and Civilisation*, he had written that 'there is no madness except as the final instance of the work of art – the work endlessly drives madness to its limits; *where there is a work of art there is no madness*; and yet madness is contemporary with the work of art, since it inaugurates its time of truth' (*MC* p. 274). This relationship between art and madness – not a dialectical relation, but the mark of a discursive limit – is an enduring idea in Foucault's writing on literature. Indeed, in an interview published in April 1964, Roland Barthes said that 'Michel Foucault has begun to speak of the Reason/Unreason couple' as 'ultimately the essential subject of all theoretical work on literature'.[12]

Foucault's only full-length work dedicated to a writer is significantly a study of Raymond Roussel, a little-remembered prose and verse writer, a contemporary of Proust, who had experienced ecstatic hallucinatory visions as a young man, and had later received treatment from the renowned psychologist Pierre Janet. (Janet's *De l'angoisse à l'extase*, 1926, is a published case history of Roussel.) The book, entitled simply *Raymond Roussel* in French, was translated into English as *Death and the Labyrinth*.

Foucault argues in *Death and the Labyrinth* that the hollowness of death is at the centre of the intricate series of puns, slips and word play that constitute the self-referential textuality of Raymond Roussel. Roussel's prose-writing process took three potential forms. In the first, he would end a narrative passage with a phrase repeating the sounds, but not the meaning, of the passage's opening phrase. In the second, he created a passage by selecting two words, each with a double meaning, then placing the proposition 'à' between them, linking the first phrase to the second. In the third, he took a random and inconsequential phrase or expression and transformed it into a similar-sounding phrase, with wholly different meaning, around which a situation could be constructed. This process, for Foucault, constituted a hidden system in which the repetition, randomness and limitedness of Roussel's language indicates the extent to which 'verbal signs' are themselves empty of meaning. The limited void of language reflects an ontological void: Roussel's complex strategies with language reveal the 'absolute emptiness of being that he must surround, dominate and overwhelm with pure invention' (*DL*, p. 17). Language illustrates the limitations and emptiness of the idea of subject, because *it too* is revealed to be limited and empty.

Language is also given a spatial dimension in Roussel. His texuality is seen as an experiment in 'constructing and criss-crossing the two great mythic spaces so often explored by Western imagination' (*DL*, p. 80). These are labyrinthine spaces: 'space that is rigid and forbidden, surrounding the quest, the return and the treasure'; and the space of metamorphosis: 'the other space – communicating, polymorphous, continuous, and irreversible' (*DL*, p. 80). Foucault argues that Roussel's works mark not so much the failure of the quest as the way in the notion of quest is epistemologically flawed. Thus, any search for a myth of origins is revealed as fundamentally empty, and the supposed origin is revealed to be identical with its effects.

Once syntax and narrative structure are so fully emptied out, Roussel's literary language becomes for Foucault a marker or talisman of our mortality. In his critical work on Foucault and literature, Simon During points out the distinction between the project of the structuralists to assert the primacy of the text, and Foucault's metaphysical reflection on language and mortality:

> It might be enough to say that in *Death and the Labyrinth*, Foucault's 'theme' has become language itself, its limits and its relation to the world. However, let us recall that Foucault is not thinking of 'language' as the structuralists were to conceive of it – as a system able to produce effects of signification (a welding together of signified and signifier) by means of a network of repetitions, differences and substitutions. Rather language for Foucault here begins to take the form ascribed to it within poststructuralism: it is *not* an autonomous and bounded system but a fold within the world, another set of things characterised by what Paul de Man called 'spacing'. It constitutes a condition delicately balanced between the ontological and the experiential: that is, a condition of Being as lived in an interval between a birth that cannot be remembered and a death that will never be experienced or concretely foreseen.[13]

Literary language for Foucault, then, as exemplified by Roussel in Foucault's account, is the material trace of the specific conditions of our existence in time and in space.

In an essay entitled 'Language to Infinity', originally published in *Tel Quel* in 1963, Foucault articulates the relationship between language and death slightly differently. We write, as Blanchot comments, so as not to die. By describing tragedies and misfortunes in literary form, we seek to open up the distance between ourselves and them. However, Foucault writes: 'Boundless misfortune [...] marks the point where language begins; but the limit of death opens before language, or rather within language, an infinite space' (*EW ii*, p. 90). Trying to distance itself from mortality, language comes face to face with itself in 'a play of mirrors that has no limits' (*EW ii*, p. 90). Foucault argues here that whereas in the Homeric epic the hero's hermetic story, erected for his immortal glory, kept mortality disingenuously at bay, modern writing, exemplified by Sade, Kafka and Borges, 'has moved infinitely closer to its source, to this disquieting sound which announces from the depth of language – once we attend to it – the source against which we seek refuge and toward which we address ourselves' (*EW ii*, p. 94).

Modern literature is caught in the impossible task of trying to name all, to represent exhaustively. It therefore risks becoming unreadable, as Sade's pornography is 'unreadable' according to Foucault. Produced in confinement, and circling eternally around its own extreme repetitions of ritualistic sexual acts, Sade's texts enact an impossible *mise-en-abyme* of representation. The interest of Sade for Foucault lies not in the *content* of his erotica but in the function that its form fulfils: 'the precise object of "sadism" is not the other, neither his body nor his sovereignty: it is everything that might have been said' (*EW ii*, p. 96). Trying to say everything, language repeats itself infinitely, coming up against its own limits in the mirror, 'but postpones death indefinitely by ceaselessly opening a space where it is always the analogue of itself' (*EW ii*, p. 100). This notion of a modern literature as endlessly recycling textual repetitions offers a prescient account of theories of literature in post-modernism.

As an afterword to these comments on Foucault's reading of Sade, it is worth pointing out that despite his interest in the scopic, as well as the literary, Foucault made a substantial commentary on cinematic art only once. His interview with Gérard Dupont published in *Cinématographie* in 1975, entitled 'Sade: Sergeant of Sex', concerns the feasibility of adapting for the screen the writings of the 'divine Marquis', and questions the 'sadism' of filmic representations produced in the 1970s. Foucault comments provocatively that 'there can be nothing more allergic to the cinema than the work of Sade' (*EW ii*, p. 223). He claims this on the grounds that the ritual and ceremonial nature of the content and structure of Sade's pornography, its closed world of 'carefully programmed regulation', excludes the possibility of creative, certainty-shattering image-making, of the 'supplementary play of the camera' (*EW ii*, p. 223). Foucault describes Sade, in a memorable formula, as 'an accountant of the ass and its equivalents' (*EW ii*, p. 223), evoking that which makes Sade sit on the cusp of the moderns for Foucault: his tireless attempt to represent when the possibility of meaningful representation has been exhausted, and his belonging within a disciplinary model of sex (more of this in chapter 6) which excludes imaginative possibilities of pleasure outside of regimented meanings.

Foucault argues that provocative filmmaking of the 1970s, such as Alejandro Jodorowsky's *El Topo* or Werner Schroeter's *The Death of Maria Malibran*, which the interviewer suggests to him may be described as 'sadistic', is in fact very far from meriting this label, 'except through the detour of a vague psychoanalysis involving a partial object, a body in pieces, the *vagina dentata*' (*EW ii*, p. 224). In filming practice such as Schroeter's, Foucault argues, 'there is an anarchizing of the body, in which hierarchies, localizations and designations, organicity if you like, is being undone' and 'the goal is to dismantle [. . .] organicity' (*EW ii*, p. 224). This is in stark contrast to the understanding of (psychological rather than literary) sadism that Foucault introduces here, in which 'it's very much the organ as such that it relentlessly targeted. You have an eye that looks. I tear it from you. You have a tongue that I have taken between my lips and bitten, I'm going to cut it off. With this tongue you will no longer be able to eat or speak' (*EW ii*, p. 224). Foucault's notion of the 'new' cinematic body in Schroeter's film as abstracting from its own organicity resembles very closely

Deleuze and Guattari's conception of the body as a desiring machine, or a body without organs.[14] This 'machine' is productive of multiple libidinous desires, rather than susceptible to the model of desire as lack; a psychoanalytic model in which desire is always exacerbated and eternally thwarted. Just as the unified subject disappears in *avant garde* writing for Foucault, so the organised body is subject to dissolution in *avant garde* filming. Identity, once again, is that which is to be erased.

Author functions

Despite the number of words he devoted to studying the production of *avant garde* authors (and some critics' claims that these authors' lifestyles and identities – as gay or mad – fascinated him as much as their textuality),[15] Foucault ultimately advises caution regarding the project of literary criticism, and particularly biographical criticism. Foucault's suspicion of biographical criticism is in evidence as early as 1962, with his Introduction to Jean-Jacques Rousseau's *Dialogues*. Here he displays an interest in Rousseau's problematisation of his own quest to represent himself authentically and truthfully via *The Confessions*, which were to be published only posthumously to avoid revealing the scandalous self during the author's lifetime. However, inevitably they produced rumour, a 'quasi secrecy' (*EW ii*, p. 34), owing to Rousseau's tendency to read them aloud to friends at social gatherings. Foucault also discusses the inevitable and simultaneous existence/distinction of 'Jean-Jacques' (the private man) and 'Rousseau' (the author name) in the published *Dialogues*. Foucault expresses the impossibility of the two names ever completely merging in the presence of writing.

It is, however, in 'What is an Author?' that Foucault articulates clearly and cogently his suspicion of the interpretative reading method known in Anglo-American criticism as 'the man and his works'; a suspicion that he also alluded to in a much more lyrical and opaque style in his essays on Bataille and Blanchot, where he insisted on the prevalence of the word over the subjectivity of the author. 'What is an Author?' argues that, if we use the author's biography to interpret the meaning of the body of works s/he has produced, we impose a false coherence upon these works.

The very notion of the author is, Foucault argues, a construction proper to the 'privileged moment of individualization in the history of ideas, knowledge, literature, philosophy and the sciences' (*EW ii*, p. 205). Developing his ideas on the link between writing and death that we have seen expressed in *Death and the Labyrinth* and 'Language to Infinity', Foucault argues that the modern writer has worked to efface every trace of his identity from the text, such that 'he must assume the role of the dead man in the game of writing' (*EW ii*, p. 207). Foucault goes on to posit that the 'death of the author', proclaimed by Roland Barthes in 1967, has allowed for a critical shift in emphasis from the producer of a text to the text itself. This turn towards the text is, of course, a major tenet of both the hermeneutic tradition and literary structuralism, and continued to retain its importance for such post-structuralist critics as Paul de Man and Derrida. However, Foucault highlights a certain problem that remains despite the shift towards considering 'the work' rather than the author. The definition of 'work' is itself problematic, as it is not immediately clear what constitutes a 'work' and how a work might exist in the absence of an author identity. For example, Sade's prison scribblings on rolls of parchments only became 'works' (capable of being canonised in France's prestigious *Pléiade* series) once Sade's status as author was recognised. Simultaneously, Foucault asks, how do we decide what constitutes the 'works' of a given author? Should Nietzsche's laundry list be included in an edition of his complete works along with his early drafts of essays and plans for his aphorisms? If not, why not? What arbitrary value judgements and cultural codes are coming into play when we make such decisions?

Foucault's aim here is to highlight how the notion of the work and the notion of the author are at once interdependent and unstable, and more fundamentally, how they persist in our way of imagining literature, even if the critical consensus of his time happily followed Barthes in proclaiming the author dead. Foucault goes on to explain how the author's name has functioned differently at given moments of history. In the ancient world, any medical text endowed with authority would be attributed to the name 'Hippocrates', without the man Hippocrates having to have voiced, dictated or physically inscribed it. Thus, 'the author's name manifests the appearance of a certain discursive set and indicates the status of this discourse within a society and a culture' (*EW ii*, p. 211). Moreover, 'in a civilization like our own there are a certain number of discourses endowed with the "author function" while others are deprived of it' (*EW ii*, p. 211). To illustrate this, Foucault points out that a private letter or a legal contract bears a signature, but this person's name is not given the status of 'author'. Conversely, the function of the author's name is central to our reception and canonization of texts such as those that say 'Shakespeare'. Thus, a series of cultural values is invisibly in play whenever authorship is evoked and an author function attributed to a text.

This idea of the 'author function' is the concept that Foucault develops to relativise and denaturalise for us the role of 'authorship' in our cultural consciousness. He goes on to point out that one function of named authorship towards the end of the eighteenth and in the early nineteenth centuries was to attribute responsibility (which increasingly gained juridico-legal significance) to an individual for the works s/he authored. Hence, says Foucault, the author's relationship to transgression has always been a particular one. Recognition and ownership is one side of the coin of authorship, of which the other side is prohibition and punishment. Authors such as Baudelaire and Flaubert, prosecuted for outraging morality in the middle of the nineteenth century, thus bore the burden as well as the privilege of having their names function as 'authors'.

Fundamentally, argues Foucault, 'this author function [...] does not develop spontaneously as the attribution of a discourse to an individual. It is, rather, the result of a complex operation that constructs a certain being of reason that we call "author"' (*EW ii*, p. 213). This 'being of reason' is the means by which we establish unity within a 'body of work' belonging to the same author. We search, says Foucault, for enduring motifs and obsessions, and for signs of maturation and development through the chronological course of the opus.

Foucault goes on in the final section of his essay to examine those cases where the scope of the 'author function' is broadened beyond the attribution of a certain literary work to a certain famous name. There are also, he states, authors of theories, ideas and trends. These author names, such as Freud and Marx (and, arguably, Foucault), are more than authors – they are 'founders of discursivity' (*EW ii*, p. 217). These 'transdiscursive' authors make possible more than could be made possible by any novelist. Whereas Ann Radcliffe makes possible the generic conditions for the production of other gothic novels (that is she generates the possibility of analogy), the author name 'Freud' does more than inspire Melanie Klein and Karl Abraham to build other works of psychoanalysis. Freud creates the conditions for *divergences* from his own work that nonetheless refer to and arise from the discursive field of psychoanalysis. Foucault thereby differentiates the foundation of a discourse from the development of a scientific theory, since, in science, the initial finding is progressively modified by future work, and the original act of foundation is not reified as originary or authoritative. Foucault writes: 'unlike the founding of a science, the initiation of a discursive practice does not participate in its later transformations' (*EW ii*, p. 219). The construction of the idea of a founder or originator of a theoretical framework, such as Freud or Marx, creates the conditions by which we seek to authorise all future pronouncements within the 'field', referring them back to the origin, either as additions to or refutations of the 'original' theory.

The conclusion of Foucault's essay sets out the reasons why the study of the author function is politically important. Foucault argues that looking at the ways in which the figure constructed as the originator of a discourse functions offers a better insight into the cultural status of that discourse than would an analysis of its content or 'expressive value' (*EW ii*, p. 220). Secondly, analysis of the author function offers a way into re-examining more generally 'the privileges of the subject' in discourse (*EW ii*, p. 220). Finally, Foucault argues that an analysis of the workings of author function dispels the myth of the individual man of genius, by which authority and significance are accorded to certain texts and not to others. Contrary to what we are told, 'the author is not an indefinite source of significations that fill a work; the author does not precede the works; he is a certain functional principle by which, in our culture, one limits, excludes, and chooses; in short, by which one limits the free circulation, the free manipulation, the free composition, decomposition and recomposition of fiction' (*EW ii*, p. 221). Foucault concludes that the figure of the author is ideological, in so far as he actually functions in the opposite way to that in which he appears to function. In attributing the proliferation of signification and the transcendence of genius to the individual author, we in fact stem the productiveness and creativity of multiple voices, controlling and narrowing the production of culture. Foucault ends on a prophetic note, by predicting that 'as our society changes, at the very moment when it is in the process of changing, the author function will disappear' (*EW ii*, p. 222). He proposes that instead of asking questions regarding the originality, authenticity and fidelity of discursive pronouncements in relation to their founding statements, we would ask instead:

> What are the modes of existence of this discourse? Where has it been used, how can it circulate, and who can appropriate it for himself? What are the places in it where there is room for possible subjects? Who can assume these various subject functions? And behind all these questions, we would hear hardly anything but the stirring of an indifference: what difference does it make who is speaking.
>
> (*EW ii*, p. 222)

Evacuating the original authorial personality from the analysis of discourse would enable a truer and more critical apprehension of its operation.

We may not have arrived quite yet at the utopian moment that Foucault imagines here. However, in 1980, Foucault himself attempted to demonstrate the power of the anonymity of the authorial voice to the reading public when he consented to give an interview to the newspaper *Le Monde*, which was running a weekly series of discussions with leading intellectual figures, but refused to be named as the subject of the interview. When the interviewer asks why his interviewee has chosen anonymity, the latter responds in the following terms:

In our societies, characters dominate our perceptions. Our attention tends to be arrested by the activities of faces that come and go, emerge and disappear.

Why did I suggest that we use anonymity? Out of nostalgia for a time when, being quite unknown, what I said had some chance of being heard. With the potential reader, the surface of contact was unrippled. The effects of the book might land in unexpected places and form shapes that I had never thought of. A name makes reading too easy.

(*EW* i, p. 321)

Conclusion

The broader implications of Foucault's ideas concerning the author function deployed in 'What is an Author?' have to do with his ongoing attempt to rethink the functioning of discourse. Using literary production and the workings of the author name as a concrete example, Foucault gives specificity and substance to his contention in *The Archaeology of Knowledge* that the subject does not play the role of the 'originator' of discourse, but that the very idea of the subject is produced as an *effect* of the functioning of impersonal and automatic discursive operations. Foucault's attraction to authors such as Blanchot and Roussel, for example, rests on the fact that in the works of these authors, the subjective voice is often blurred, pluralised, ambiguous or absent, meaning that the only subject of language is language itself. At the end of *The Order of Things*, Foucault had made the point that the erasure of the category of 'man' that he predicted as the correlative of a future epistemic shift was already, presciently, internal to the writings of such *avant gardistes*:

> From within language experienced and traversed as language, in the play of its possibilities extended to their furthest point, what emerges is that man has 'come to an end', and that, by reaching the summit of all possible speech, he arrives not at the very heart of himself but at the brink of that which limits him [. . .] it was inevitable that this new mode of being of literature should have been revealed in works like those of [. . .] Roussel.

(*OT*, p. 419)

Thus, for Foucault, texts such as these reveal in exemplary fashion the functioning of language to illustrate the absence of the subject that humanistic discourse habitually occludes. Similarly, where his *History of Madness* was heavily criticised for having suggested that the voice of unreason may have contained, prior to its institutionalisation in psychiatry, the capacity to challenge rational discourse, the concrete example of literary language and its subject dissolving and dispersing on the page allows Foucault to demonstrate the power of an anti-rational, anti-individualistic impulse. It is for these reasons that Foucault's body of writing about literature is a fundamental, significant, and unfortunately often overlooked aspect of his corpus. Via his discussion of literature, he is able to articulate some of the critiques of Western thinking that his archaeological histories of medicine and knowledge achieved only partially, controversially, and at the cost of a good deal of negative criticism.

The Foucaldian literary-critical method operates, then, at a meta-level. Rather than asking questions directly about the author and his or her works, he encourages us to ask questions about the way the author function operates to reflect or promote the meanings and values of the containing culture. One can argue that a Foucaldian approach is crucial to the dynamism of literary studies, as it allows critics to reflect upon the presuppositions and cultural-historical conditions of their methods and promotes the interdisciplinary approach that has renovated subjects in the arts and humanities in recent years.

As a final word, we have seen that what is at stake for Foucault in thinking about literature is, again, the question of the self: the self that is historically located; that is not fixed; that reinvents itself as it disappears from focus. The self that is not an author (as institution or authority) but an author *function*; a historically contingent construction; a creation of culture rather than a 'natural' being with innate genius. Literary language is important for Foucault because it is language working at the limits of expression, language that pushes us to witness the shattering of the fiction of the self and the prevalence of historical process and reinvention. At the end of his career, Foucault will reflect upon the ethical and aesthetic conditions necessary for self-creation, for self-stylisation and for an art of pleasure. First, it seems, he needed to demonstrate the complete erasure of selfhood through extreme literary language, the death of the existential ego – a concept of self that dominated his intellectual environment – in order to imagine new possibilities for philosophy and experience.

Works: crime and punishment

Prison has the advantage of producing delinquency, an instrument of control over and pressure on illegality, a substantial component in the exercise of power over bodies, an element of that physics of power which gave rise to the psychology of the subject.

Michel Foucault

This chapter will explore in depth two works on criminality and regimes of discipline. *I, Pierre Rivière, Having Killed My Mother, My Sister and My Brother: A Case of Parricide in the Nineteenth Century* (1973) is a collection of legal and medical reports, accompanied by a long and extraordinarily detailed written confession by a French peasant who, in 1835, murdered his mother and siblings. The documents are edited and commented on by Foucault and his team of sociological researchers. Foucault's interest in the case lay in its susceptibility to be read according to the method of genealogical research he adapts and borrows from his readings of Nietzsche (see pp. 12–16 of the present book), which proceeds from the postulate that knowledge is produced as the effect of local operations of power. The case of Rivière afforded the opportunity to reflect upon the ways in which the murderer became the ground for a discursive battle between and among the contemporary medico-legal disciplines. It is a good example of Foucault's notion that force fields of discourse constitute individuals according to discrete categories of social subject, in this case criminal/medical categories.

In *Discipline and Punish* (1975), Foucault can be seen to return to the kind of politicised history of power and institutions that characterised his early works on mental illness and medicine. This time, the focus is on the carceral system: punishment and prison. Foucault himself has stated that the schism that is often insisted on by critics between his early archaeological work and later genealogical studies is in fact less deep than it may appear: 'I ask myself what else it was I was talking about in *Madness and Civilisation* or *The Birth of the Clinic* but power' (*EW iii*, p. 117). However, it is undeniable that in *Discipline and Punish*, Foucault sharpens his tools for analysing the means by which the body is made to conform to the utilitarian ends of social regimes thanks to the operations of disciplinary power. This constitutes, then, the first full-length work in the genealogical mould, announced by the short analysis presented in *I, Pierre Rivière*, and it prepares the way for Foucault's major exposition of the ways in which modern bodies are subject to the subtle workings of power in the first volume of *The History of Sexuality* a year later.

Pierre Rivière: peasant and parricide

In the course of their inquiries into the formation of the disciplines in the early 1970s, Foucault and his research team undertook archival research in an attempt to establish the history of the relationship between alienism (the precursor of modern psychiatry) and the contemporary criminal justice system. However, instead of publishing a comprehensive historical thesis on this subject, such as Foucault had produced on the birth of the clinic and would go on to produce on the birth of the prison, they published instead an edited 'dossier' of documents pertaining to just one murder case, that of Pierre Rivière, a peasant who, in 1835, murdered his mother, sister and brother, and produced a detailed written account of his family history and a confession of his crime. The dossier presented by Foucault *et al.* in 1973 consisted of three medical reports, each of which reached different conclusions about Rivière's mental state, and each produced by a practitioner with a different status in the medical profession: the first report was by a country doctor, the second by an urban physician and the third was co-signed by the leading alienists and physicians of the day. These included Esquirol, famous for having produced the diagnosis of monomania in the 1800s, and Orfila, who testified extensively as a forensic specialist in murder trials throughout the nineteenth century, including the high-profile case of husband-poisoner Marie Lafarge in 1840, cited as the first example of a forensic toxocological murder investigation. The dossier also included numerous legal documents and exhibits, mainly witness statements from the trial. Thirdly, it included Rivière's long and detailed autobiographical memoir. The case file on Rivière was the thickest of all those Foucault's team came across in the archive, and its dramatic and surprising nature – the lucid literary account penned by a peasant generally thought in his village to be illiterate – drew the attention of the team of researchers. So unusual was the case, in fact, and so striking the published dossier, that in 1976 director René Allio made a film based on the case of Rivière, one of a series of filmic meditations on rural France.

The documents in Foucault's dossier are sandwiched between a brief preface by Foucault, which explains the reasons for the team's interest in the case, and a series of short essays by each member of the research team, with which the book concludes. It is an unusual document, intended, in Foucault's words, to present to the reader 'an event that provided the intersection of discourses that differed in origin, form, organization, and function' (*IPR*, p. x). That is, it shows the impossibility of understanding the events of 1835 from any one, neutral perspective or as a phenomenon with one single meaning. It shows how acts that are criminalised become inevitably the stuff of debate, power struggles and multiple interpretations by the authority discourses that seek to establish territory in relation to them. The dossier is intended to be 'a map' (*IPR*, p. xi) of the series of debates and conflicts for which the crime provided a locus. These included debates within the medical sphere surrounding insanity pleas and the status of the monomania diagnosis; within the legal sphere, as lawyers sought to accommodate within existing law the unusual set of extenuating circumstances; among the villagers trying to overcome the horror and stigma of a massacre committed in their midst, and, lastly, a conflict within and about Pierre Rivière, centring on the tension between the madness suggested by his act and by his insistence that God had told him to commit the murders on the one hand, and the capacity for rationality and organised thought suggested by the production of his long, reasoned confessional memoir on the other. In embodying this series of debates and conflicts, in staging this confrontation between a series of authority discourses and 'lay' opinions and testimonies, the collection of documents discovered by Foucault and his team provided them with an exemplary illustration of the functioning of power relations; 'a battle among discourses and through discourses' (*IPR*, p. x).

The broader function that Foucault hoped the dossier would serve was one of 'furnishing an example of existing records that are available for potential analysis' (*IPR*, p. xi). It becomes clear that Foucault is recommending both a broadening of the *kinds of material* that should be exploited for the analysis of discourse and a *methodology* for carrying out this historical discursive analysis. Describing the approach taken to the memoirs of Rivière, Foucault writes:

> As to Rivière's discourse, we decided not to interpret it and subject it to any psychiatric or psychoanalytic commentary. In the first place because it was what we used as the zero benchmark to gauge the distance between the other discourses and the relations arising among them. Secondly, because we could hardly speak of it without involving it in one of the discourses (medical, legal, psychological, criminological) which we wished to use as our starting point in talking about it. If we had done so, we should have brought it within the power relation whose reductive effects we wished to show, and we ourselves should have fallen into the trap it set.
>
> (*IPR*, p. xiii)

I Pierre Rivière, then, is understandable as Foucault's attempt to showcase a genuinely innovative method for dealing with the kind of discursive material that would typically be subject to what Foucault would consider to be a reductive reading, pursued in the name of the psychoanalytic or psychological drive for interpretation and diagnosis. He seeks to isolate a method of reading that is not concerned with pathologising the murderer/writer or his act, but with bringing to the surface the means by which confessional discourse functions to mobilise and orient other discourses, giving rise to a set of interpretations that weave wars of pathology and taxonomy around their subject matter, in a battle of authority disciplines. This method, then, makes a clever and typically Foucaldian gesture of turning interpretative focus away from the marginalised, abnormal, othered subject and on to the dominant disciplinary frameworks by which such subjects are usually interpreted. It makes into the object of study those very discourses that habitually pronounce upon others from a privileged subject position.

The Pierre Rivière dossier also provides Foucault with material for sketching a short history of the construction of the figure of the murderer and the function of murderers' confessions, in his contribution to the short set of essays following the edited documents, entitled 'Tales of Murder'. Here he argues that the confessions produced by Rivière have an interesting status in as much as they were interpreted as two facets of the same act: 'the fact of killing and the fact of writing, the deeds done and the things narrated, coincided since they were elements of a like nature' (*IPR*, p. 200). The text, then, became an extension of the crime, to the extent that the rationality of the confessions gave rise to suppositions regarding the sanity of the criminal and the premeditated nature of his act. Foucault goes on to show how Rivière's case throws into question the whole notion of premeditation: 'in Rivière's behavior memoir and murder were not ranged simply in chronological sequence – crime and then narrative. The text does not relate directly to the deed; a whole web of relations is woven between the one and the other' (*IPR*, p. 201).

Rivière himself elaborated three potential projects which would offer differing chronological/logical relationships between the memoir and the crime; the conception and the act. First, he could write the memoir announcing the murder, then commit the murder, then mail the memoir, then kill himself. Secondly, he could write a text about his parents' life in which the murder remained a secret until the end, then kill as the culminating act. Thirdly, he could kill first, be caught, then write the memoir, then die. But in this third case, the memoir would be already written in his head before the crime, awaiting the moment when it could be poured on to paper. The *conception* of the memoir would, in a sense, give rise to the killing. The third sequence is closest to what actually happened; however, the three different narrative versions of the chronology and causality of a crime and its retelling allow for an effective collapsing of any easy supposition that an act comes first and is then simply recorded; a murder planned and then carried out with detailed precision. Instead the murder gets moved around in the (re)construction that the killer/ writer attempts here. Indeed, it seems that Rivière waited a long time before agreeing to write his memoir for the legal examination. By withholding confession, and then using it to throw into question the whole teleology of cause and event, motivation and act, Rivière offers Foucault the opportunity to argue almost *literally* for 'the equivalence weapon/discourse' (*IPR*, p. 203) that Foucault identifies not only in the case of murder, but as a principle governing social relations in general. In this model, words are the very stuff of power struggles, not just the tools for describing them; words are arms for waging the eternal battle of knowledge, confession and resistance.

Comments on *I Pierre Rivière . . .*

Subsequent commentators upon Foucault's editing of *I Pierre Rivière* have drawn attention to a problem in the treatment of the case, a problem often mentioned in connection with Foucault's analyses in general. It is a certain blind spot with regard to gender politics and a resistance to spotting the misogyny underlying discourses, a feature that is especially noticeable given that other instances of power relations are so closely and expertly analysed.[1] The gender politics of the discursive treatment of the crime described are completely ignored. The 'parricide' in question was the killing of Pierre's mother and two siblings, not his father, since – as he explicitly states – he wanted to free himself and his father from the tyranny of the wife/mother. The term 'parricide', with its Latin prefix meaning 'kin', means in nineteenth-century law simply to kill a parent; however, this labelling renders invisible the gendered specificity of the killing in Pierre Rivière's case. The essay by Blandine Barret-Kriegel at the end of *I Pierre Rivière*, 'Regicide and Parricide', looks in detail at the close links between the crime of killing a sovereign and that of killing one's parents, since the institution of the family represents social order and hierarchy in the microcosm. Moreover, links were made at the time between the case of Rivière, tried in 1835, and the contemporaneous trial of the regicide Fieschi. However, the link between crown and family, parricide and regicide, clearly rests on a relation between *paternal* authority and sovereign power. Rivière's killing of his mother signifies quite differently at the level of the symbolic attack on authority than the murder of his father would have done. The failure of any member of the team of collaborators to analyse this salient fact does suggest quite strongly that questions of gender politics were not at the centre of Foucault's interests. Given Foucault's explicit refusal to put Rivière's crime into a psychoanalytic framework, one can see perhaps why this might lead to an avoidance of any discussion of the symbolic 'meaning' of killing the mother or killing the father. An Oedipal interpretation may suggest itself rather too readily once one has embarked on such an investigation. However, an analysis of the gendering of the discourses surrounding parricide and the forces of gendered power at work here would not have transgressed the tenets of Foucault's methodology, and might have lent another dimension to the genealogical treatment of Rivière's case.

Another critique one could level at Foucault's rhetoric in this text is the problem of the extent to which he obviously felt seduced by the writing voice of Rivière, and his repeated ascription of aesthetic qualities to the murderer's memoir. He admits that the main reason that the team spent so long working on the dossier was 'simply the beauty of Rivière's memoir' (*IPR*, p. x). And later: 'its beauty alone is sufficient justification for it today' (*IPR*, p. 199). As well as aestheticising Rivière's text, Foucault ascribes to it awesome and bewitching powers: 'owing to a sort of reverence and perhaps, too, terror for a text which was to carry off four corpses along with it, we were unwilling to superimpose our own text upon Rivière's memoir. We fell under the spell of the parricide with the reddish-brown eyes' (*IPR*, p. xiii). Such comments suggest a discourse very close to the nineteenth-century Romantic discourse of the criminal genius or poet-murderer.[2] As is often the case in Foucault's writing, it is not entirely clear whether this discourse is being deliberately evoked and pastiched, or whether the attraction suggested in Foucault's words is to be read at face value here. It is a puzzling feature of the text: for such an arch-demystifier of discursive constructions, maintaining the power of the aesthetic criminal would be an intriguing and uncharacteristic lapse: a surprising glimpse, perhaps, of Foucault's personal tastes and fancies which push through the surface of the analytical text.

Punishing the body and soul

In Alan Sheridan's 1977 translation of *Surveiller et Punir* as *Discipline and Punish*, he makes the following comments about the difficulty of accurately rendering the title in English: 'the verb "surveiller" has no adequate English equivalent [. . .] In the end Foucault himself suggested *Discipline and Punish*, which relates closely to the book's structure' (*DP*, n.p.). What is missing from this translation, albeit suggested by Foucault, is the importance of spectacle and the role of the visual in the operations of power and punishment, an idea that is amply carried by the French verb *surveiller* (conveying most closely, 'observation' rather than 'surveillance'), and which is central to Foucault's analysis of the history of the carceral system.

Indeed, *Discipline and Punish* opens with a colourful and very visual account of the violent public torture and execution of the attempted regicide, Robert Damiens, in 1757. The size and enthusiasm of the attendant crowd and the theatrical exposition of the brutal bodily punishment inflicted on Damiens are treated expansively and in detail in the text. The man is drawn and quartered, literally torn apart by four horses, as well as being gouged, lacerated and dismembered by the executioner. Foucault's prose is suspenseful and unflinching, such that the dramatic scene retains some of its theatricality in the retelling. The text then moves to a dry enumeration of the timetabled activities of prisoners in a Parisian house of correction eighty years later, detailing exhaustively the daily movements of the inmates, from rising and dressing in silence at 6 a.m. and engaging in morning prayers through to a regimented bedtime routine at 7.30 p.m. in summer and 8.30 p.m. in winter. The writing style in this opening section is particularly noteworthy, as it switches from hyperbolic prose in the excruciating description of the torture to a flat, emotionless tone when listing the monotonous routine of the incarcerated inmates. As is so often the case (although this is not particularly widely acknowledged in Foucault criticism), Foucault is a keen exponent of literary and rhetorical language to mark and enact emotively and rhythmically the transitions and discontinuities his works seek to identify.[3]

Having painted his two portraits of very different 'penal styles', employed less than a century apart, Foucault explains that they announce a historical shift which may be described as the movement from the punishment of the body to the punishment of the soul (even though in the second mode, the body also remained constrained by a system of incarceration). This Enlightenment innovation is described as a 'moral technology', designed, according to Foucault, not to liberate but to control more exactly and insidiously. It is argued that the disappearance of punishment as a public spectacle at the end of the eighteenth and beginning of the nineteenth century came about not because of an increasing liberalisation or humanitarianism but rather because the 'rite that "concluded the crime" was suspected of being in some undesirable way linked with it' (*DP*, p. 9). By this, Foucault means that public displays of torture underlined the similarity between the violent nature of crime and the cold-blooded and equally brutal character of the act of punishment, linking the deeds of common murderers with the practices of state retribution embodied in the figure of the torturer or executioner. The dual effect of this could be to instil in the watching crowd a sympathy for the martyred prisoner, and to turn the 'legal violence of the executioner into shame' (*DP*, p. 9). Foucault goes on to posit that the diminishment of torture has marked a system of punishment in which the state representative no longer prolongs bodily contact with the wrongdoer. Even in the case of modern Western execution methods, by the electric chair or lethal injection, death is quick and pain is short-lived. Similarly, a uniformity of punishment has characterised the shift of system. All criminals condemned to death are subject to the same method of execution, unlike in earlier centuries, when the torture and putting to death of, for example, a regicide had to follow a set of strict and ritualised stages and practices, which would differ from the execution method meted out to the perpetrator of another type of crime.

However, the disappearance of physical torture as public spectacle and the reduction of pain in punishment do not ensure the complete disappearance of torture. Foucault claims that 'there remains a trace of "torture" in the modern mechanisms of criminal justice' (*DP*, p. 16). This would be a 'non-corporal punishment', and instead the torture would target 'the soul'. In a gesture that anticipates his comments on the social shift from understanding acts of sodomy as religious sins to the creation of the homosexual as a type of medical and social subject in *The Will to Knowledge* (see chapter 6 of the present book), Foucault argues that the judgment of individual crimes as 'juridical objects', with accompanying appropriate punishments, was eclipsed in modernity by an exploration of the nature of the perpetrator's 'passions, instincts, anomalies, infirmities, maladjustments, effects of environment or heredity [. . .]

aggressivity [...] perversions [...] drives and desires' (*DP*, p. 17). The argument here is a subtle and important one. As well as punishing acts, the penal system becomes a way of naming, judging, isolating and controlling the 'shadows lurking behind the case itself' (*DP*, p. 17). Foucault's principal and all-pervasive interest in the making of the modern self as a subject of – and as subject to – interrogation, knowledge and classification by the medical, legal and psychological sciences is at the heart of this analysis of the redefinition of criminality in modernity. In this light, the turn to rehabilitation becomes not a matter of humanitarian altruism, or the shadow of a Christian belief in the potential righteousness of all human beings, but rather a pragmatic means of supervising the *internal nature* of the criminal individual, in order to neutralise his anti-social instincts; to eliminate dissident difference. By making crime not simply a punishable act but a phenomenon to be investigated and its causes understood, with the mitigating factors of insanity to be taken into account when establishing punishment, it becomes a linchpin of the technologies for organising and ordering the modern population.

Foucault's four principles for understanding the history of the carceral system are as follows:

(1) Punishment is a complex social function, not just a means of 'repression'.
(2) Punishment must be understood as a political strategy alongside other political strategies of knowledge and control.
(3) The history of penal law and of the human sciences need to be understood as operating in tandem, as facets of each other.
(4) The punishment of the soul rather than (just) the body of the offender needs to be understood in the context of the transformation of the way in which the body is subject to and affected by the operations of power. One must understand punishment as 'situated in a certain "political economy of the body"' (*DP*, p. 25).

This final point is perhaps the most significant. Rather than analysing the genealogy of the prison system against the backdrop of a history of institutions or moral precepts, Foucault undertakes to discuss it in the context of a history of the body and of bodily politics. This marks a significant shift in his focus from that found in *The Order of Things* and *The Archaeology of Knowledge*, but picks up on and takes much further his sketch of the relationship between discursive power and the medical gaze in *The Birth of the Clinic*.

Foucault's politics of the body, he is keen to assert, is not a politics of straightforward control: 'the power exercised on the body is conceived not as a property but as a strategy' (*DP*, p. 26). As we have noted elsewhere, 'strategy' is a key term for Foucault. It may be understood here as a set of actions or dynamics that generate outcomes apparently indirectly, surreptitiously or in diffuse ways and that emanate from, as well as affecting, the body of the other. It is not a direct, transparent action with a single-minded aim or intentionality. Moreover, and crucially, it is not unilaterally employed by one agent to have a direct and predictable oppressive effect on another. Rather, as Foucault puts it 'power is [. . .] an effect that is manifested and sometimes extended by the position of those who are dominated' (*DP*, pp. 26–7). This model of politics and power as non-linear, unpredictable, and, not operating hierarchically from the top down, is at the heart of the genealogical understanding of history. It is a counterintuitive but seductive way of accounting for the complexity and instability of the operations of the field of power relations, where relationality is foregrounded and influence is not exerted in a vacuum. Foucault also asserts that it is a mistake to locate knowledge wherever power is in abeyance. Rather, 'power *produces* knowledge' (*DP*, p. 27), such that when we examine the history of power or knowledge, the object of our examination should most properly be 'power–knowledge relations' (*DP*, p. 27).

Docile bodies

Foucault's description of the way in which the disciplinary management of prisoners in modernity has created 'docile bodies' offers a striking and adaptable model for understanding regimes of training in other modern institutions: the school, the clinic, the army etc. Foucault opens the chapter entitled 'Docile Bodies' with a discussion of the making of the modern soldier. In pre-modern times, Foucault tells us, the soldier was recognisable by his natural characteristics: physical strength, courage, erect posture etc. Soldiers were chosen because they *already* possessed the qualities of a good and strong fighter. The modern soldier, in comparison, is a 'machine' that may be 'constructed' (*DP*, p. 135) from the raw material of any modern body. The modern soldier is the result of rigorously applied training methods; of the implementation of discipline.

The thesis of the chapter 'Docile Bodies' is that the eighteenth century saw the dawn of the conceptualisation of the body as raw material capable of being sculpted by and for the operation of power ('Man-the-Machine'). This philosophical conception of a body which, in its docility, was infinitely manipulable was mobilised by the workings of what Foucault chooses to call the 'disciplines' for political purposes, and concretised into the human machine described in the classic study by the eighteenth-century materialist philosopher Julien Offray de La Mettrie (1748).

Foucault's description of the ways in which 'the disciplines' make use of the body and make the body ready for utility is very specific about the kind of control involved. It is not a matter of controlling the whole body, but of delimiting and constraining gestures, motions, attitudes etc. These must be as efficient and economic as possible. The modality by which this control is achieved is one of a constant and unyielding influence exerted over the body: not in the crude form of enslavement or of feudalism, but in the subtle operation of modern power, as we are encouraged throughout *Discipline and Punish* to understand the term. This power is concerned with the creation of a population that is more efficient in direct proportion to its increased obedience. Here we can see clearly a quasi-Marxian argument underlying Foucault's methodology, that he will only make explicit later in the book: the docile bodies of modernity are recognisable as the workforce of high capitalism, as well as prisoners, schoolchildren and soldiers, citizens trained and moulded in the operational factories of the schools and barracks. The operation of 'political anatomy' (*DP*, p. 138) separates 'aptitude' (which is encouraged, as it is economically productive) from the capacity to exert power. This is a good description of the alienation of the worker from the means of production as described by classical Marxian analysis. Where Foucault differs from Marx in this text, however, is in his description of the insidious and multiple workings of power: emanating from plural points, and from *within* the trained social subject as well as/rather than being exercised by an identifiable, external oppressive force (the bourgeoisie, the institutions of global capitalism). In this light, it becomes clear that revolution or overthrowal are not adequate or appropriate means of resistance to the exercise of peculiarly modern techniques of control.

Foucault goes on to describe, with a self-conscious attention to detail, the ways in which societies of docile bodies are developed and function. Firstly he discusses the 'art of distributions' (*DP*, p. 141) ('l'art des répartitions', *SP*, p. 166): that is, the ways in which 'political anatomy' operates spatially, by the physical distribution of docile bodily subjects. The distributions discussed are as follows: (1) *enclosure*: confinement in, for example, prisons or barracks; (2) *partitioning*: a more subtle use of space than enclosure, in which subjects are divided from each other to prevent the emergence of solidarity and community which would be detrimental to order; (3) *functional sites*: utilitarian architectural spaces within institutions at the disposal of more than one function; (4) *rank*: the arrangement into classes, groups, hierarchies of subjects within a system – a process of classification arranged spatially. The importance attributed by Foucault to space, geography and architecture in creating and controlling docile bodily subjects, then, is great and certain trends in recent social geography owe much to Foucault's insights here.

His second category is 'The control of activity', a temporal rather than spatial means of discipline, subdivided as follows: (1) the *timetable*: an agenda designed to 'establish rhythms, impose particular occupations, regulate the cycles of repetition' (*DP*, p. 149); (2) *the temporal elaboration of the act*: the regulatory rhythm and timespan of each given activity in the timetable; the pace imposed upon an activity (most concretely exemplified by the kinds of steps taken by soldiers in military marching); (3) *the correlation of the body and the gesture*: the correct – i.e. most efficient – use of the body in each timetabled activity; (4) *the body–object articulation*: the establishment of the correct relationship between the body and the objects it obligatorily wields (e.g. the soldier's hand and the gun); (5) *exhaustive use*: the efficient employment of time, ideologically coded in modernity as a positive value, but also the elimination of laziness and a means of ensuring that subjects do not have sufficient energy to pursue non-productive or transgressive endeavours.

In the third and fourth categories, 'the organisation of geneses' and 'the composition of forces', Foucault explores the ways in which the disciplines capitalise on the efficient deployment of bodies in time, and the ways in which bodies are not only *distributed* spacially and temporally, as described above, but also *composed* as components of a larger effective and functioning machine, whether a troop of soldiers strategically deployed for warfare or a high-capitalist workforce. The textual detail into which Foucault goes here to describe the very varied means by which the body is disciplined adumbrates the number and complexity of the mechanisms and emphasises Foucault's point regarding the impossibility of understanding disciplinary power as operating simply or uni-directionally.

Having established the range and variation of the means by which docile bodies are produced, Foucault concludes that military and political organisations are closely aligned from the classical age onwards in their tactical use of disciplined bodies over time and space. Foucault's interest in listing and classification, as a means of conducting an argument as well as an object of historical and systematic study (as seen in *The Order of Things*), is abundantly in evidence in this section of *Discipline and Punish*. By accumulating ample evidence of the different ways in which the body is organised, he insists upon the meticulous variation of these modes of training, which usually go unnoticed and unanalysed.

Self-surveillance: the panopticon

Foucault tells us that 'the exercise of discipline presupposes a mechanism that coerces by means of observation; an apparatus in which the techniques that make it possible to see induce effects of power, and in which, conversely, the means of coercion make those on whom they are applied clearly visible' (*DP*, p. 170). The centrality to his overall thesis of the contention that power is intimately linked to sight and to being seen reinforces my comment at the outset of this chapter that it is a pity that the title of the English translation excludes any overtones of surveillance, overseeing or observation. Similarly, what is crucial in this citation is the expression 'induce effects of power', for the means of disciplining the population – both normal and abnormal – that Foucault proposes are not about a model of oppressive power but about a series of techniques that work so as to give the impression that force is being exercised, without it being traceable to any single source. This deceptive, diffuse and plural operation of power characterises the second half of Foucault's corpus and the model of surveillance here is different from the dominant medical gaze described in *The Birth of the Clinic*, where the power is wielded by the gazing doctor over the gazed-at body, alive or dead.

In order to illustrate the changing nature of observation as a means of control through history, Foucault first refers to the measures taken in plague towns at the end of the seventeenth century. These involve spatial partitioning, quarantining the population, killing stray animals, immobilising the majority of the populace, with only a few 'syndics' permitted to move between sections of the town, and locking inhabitants into their houses. Observation posts are set up at each of the town gates and sentinels are posted at the ends of streets. Individuals are frozen in position. This results, according to Foucault, in a situation whereby 'inspection functions ceaselessly' and 'the gaze is alert everywhere' (*DP*, p. 195). It is, he states, 'the great review of the living and the dead' (*DP*, p. 196). The technologies of plague control described by Foucault function, then, as one means of establishing and ensuring an ordered and governed state: every element of the population is kept in its place by rigorous observation and policing.

Having described the means of monitoring a plague town, Foucault moves back in history to describe the control of lepers. This was achieved by the observation of a simplistic binary distinction, 'them and us', with 'them' excluded from society and completely 'othered'. The developments implemented to control the plague complexified this simple division, and gave rise to techniques of government whereby separations and partitions were multiple, and techniques of observation and control intensified. The latter technique provided the disciplinary model which the nineteenth century would perfect in the institutions of the asylum, the penitentiary and the reformatory. However, the technique of othering seen in the case of lepers continued to operate in these institutions, with the labelling of subjects as mad/sane; dangerous/harmless; normal/abnormal etc. Thus nineteenth-century power combines exclusion with multiple division; increasing the number of categories of exception and exclusion, but observing the positive/negative binary logic that practises rejection of the abnormal.

Foucault's interest in the category of the 'abnormal' is central to his genealogical project. It was during the time of writing and preparing to write *Discipline and Punish*, the academic year 1974–5, that he delivered a series of lectures at the Collège de France on the classification and development of techniques for treating abnormality, and the complex relationship between abnormality and the law, that have been transcribed and recently translated for publication into English as *Abnormal*. Foucault explains here how the subtle, modern techniques for dealing with the 'individual to be corrected' or the 'incorrigible' (*A*, p. 325) are developed 'at the same time that disciplinary techniques are being established in the army, schools, workshops, and then a little later in families themselves. The new practices for training bodies, behavior, and abilities open up the problem of those who escape a system of norms that has ceased to be that of the sovereignty of law' (*A*, p. 235).

Modern techniques of surveillance become increasingly subtle and insidious, according to Foucault, once the 'sovereignty of law' is no longer an unimpeachable given. Central to his account of the dominion of disciplinary power and the construction of a docile population is the architectural figure of Jeremy Bentham's panopticon, a structure designed to allow the constant surveillance of inmates from an 'invisible' central observation point. The panopticon isolates its inmates from each other in separate cells, ensuring that each individual can be seen from the central point, but simultaneously separating him from his neighbours, an object of observation but never a 'subject of communication' (*DP*, p. 200); effectively preventing plotting, insubordination or insurrection, since these are *communal* strategies of resistance. Foucault comments that this method provides in schools, mental institutions and prisons a laboratory for the study of individuals as well as a means of regulating their behaviour.

As the watcher cannot be seen or identified by the watched, the inmates develop an impersonal and anonymous relationship with power. Without being able to verify the presence of the watcher, they soon behave *as if they are being watched*, without knowing for certain whether or not this is the case. Thus, discipline becomes self-regulatory. Foucault states concisely that the panopticon is 'a machine for dissociating the see/being seen dyad' (*DP*, p. 202). This is a much simpler, more subtle and efficient method of control than that seen in the ordering of the seventeenth-century plague town with its heavy reliance on manpower and constant work of multiple segregation. It is the ideal operation of 'everyday' control rather than the mobilisation of forces against an extraordinary set of circumstances. The panopticon must be understood as more than just a 'dream building'; rather it is a 'figure of political technology that may and must be detached from any specific use' (*DP*, p. 205).

Foucault goes on to analyse several outcomes of this 'extension of the disciplinary institutions' (*DP*, p. 210) presaged by the operations of panopticism. Firstly, what had initially been intended to mitigate a negative situation ('fix a useless or disturbed population', *DP*, p. 210) was now being employed for 'positive' ends, to increase the utility and efficacy of the population. Secondly, the methods of control issuing from the disciplinary establishments tend to become flexible and adaptable. The example given is that Christian schools do more than simply observe the obedience of the children: they reach out to investigate the rectitude and morality of the parents, extending beyond their immediate institutional boundaries. Thirdly, the establishment of organised police forces extends beyond the control of social disorder and crime to infiltrate every tiny detail of life; their omnipresence is suggested everywhere, with the result of instilling the sense of being overseen in the populace as a constant effect.

Foucault posits, then, that modern culture is a 'disciplinary society' (*DP*, p. 216) that works analogously to Bentham's design for the panopticon, motivated and implemented by the move from 'quarantine' to the multiple and diverse operation of power in the most minute and apparently inconsequential aspects of social life: 'it may be said that the disciplines are techniques for assuring the ordering of human multiplicities' (*DP*, p. 218). The effects of disciplinary power are not exercised from a single vantage point, but are mobile, multivalent and internal to the very fabric of our everyday life.

Concluding remarks on *Discipline and Punish*

Foucault's *Discipline and Punish* is a suggestive and surprising book. Despite his own engagement with political campaigns to empower prisoners to pursue their rights, and although Foucault states that 'prisons do not diminish the crime rate' (*DP*, p. 265) (indeed he argues that prisons *create* delinquents, in so far as they categorise and isolate criminal types, constructing new social subjects), it does not seek straightforwardly to oppose the generally accepted proposition that an increased leniency and humanitarianism characterise the history of reforms of the penal and carceral systems. Indeed, this question of liberalisation *as such* does not seem to concern him much in any direct way. Instead, he demonstrates how the infiltration into the mainstream social order of techniques of discipline developed in the carceral context announces the emergence both of a new form of power that infiltrates all modern social organisations and a new social subject, the *homo docilis*, a compliant being produced as a result of the operation of the disciplines. This is a direct rejection of the Marxist assertion that power operates on and dominates only the proletarian classes. The dynamics of power described in Foucault's account are ones of internalisation, invisibility, plurality and discretion (torture is displaced from the surface of the body to the inner soul; surveillance is transformed from a matter of external overseeing to a rigorous self-policing). They also concern the division, segregation and separation of populations (whether in schools, prisons or the army) into manageable units where their energy can be deployed most effectively and obediently for productive and conformist ends. In some ways, this is a devastating critique of modern societies' invisible cruelties and constraints, rather than a plea for individual cases of 'reform' or 'rights'. Foucault asks rhetorically, in a highly politicised and memorable gesture: 'Is it surprising that prisons resemble factories, schools, barracks, hospitals, which all resemble prisons?' (*DP*, p. 228).

This gesture – perhaps inevitably given the force of its assertion and the far-reaching implications for our understanding of society if we are to accept it – has not gone unchallenged. Anthony Giddens[4] has sought to temper the totalising implications of Foucault's theory by contrasting it with Erving Goffman's more nuanced argument in *Asylums* (1961).[5] Unlike Foucault, Goffman argues for a radical difference between institutions – such as prisons and madhouses – which subject the inmate to a process of 'civil death' and those which simply teach or enforce behaviour that permits social functioning. Other critiques of Foucault's method in this work have focused on the problem that, despite nominally removing power from the operation of the agency of the subject, *Discipline and Punish* concentrates only on the way in which it is exercised on the basis of the functioning of those 'in charge' – governors, warders, even the architect. Peter Dews in particular has pointed out that no attention is paid here (unlike in the later writing on sexuality) to the power of resistance or subversion on the part of those submitted to the regimes of discipline.[6] Only official discourses of knowledge are considered, not the reverse discourses of, for example, prison sub-cultures (the popular wisdom that an inexperienced criminal will emerge from a term in prison possessed of considerably more knowledge, of a most unofficial and undisciplined kind, than he had when he went in).

These, perhaps valid, critiques notwithstanding, it is difficult not to be impressed and affected by Foucault's powerful illustrations and demonstrations of the ways in which apparently very different institutions, operating with ostensibly dissimilar aims, have the common effect of training the corporeal subject in techniques of self-control and 'good behaviour'. We are all implicated in the revelations of this analysis, as we have all been – at the very least – schoolchildren. Moreover, the powerful impact of the book's description of a panoptical society has not faded with time. As we move into an age of increasing security and surveillance, predominated by media panic regarding a ubiquitous and insidious threat of 'terrorism' produced by the divisions within our own cultures, Foucault's book, written in the mid-1970s, continues – surprisingly perhaps – to have a very real social relevance and resonance.

Chapter 6

Works: *The History of Sexuality*

> There is a significant difference between interdictions about sexuality and other forms of interdiction. Unlike other interdictions, sexual interdictions are constantly connected with the obligation to tell the truth about oneself.
>
> Michel Foucault

One of the most striking and original contributions for which Foucault is remembered is his counterintuitive contention and compelling theoretical demonstration that 'sexuality' has a history, which is constituted in the 'link between the obligation to tell the truth and the prohibitions weighing on sexuality' (*EW i*, p. 224). An erotic practice or 'preference' has not always, everywhere, been assumed to have the same significance; rather behaviours and choices that today we would understand as 'sexual' mean different things at different periods and in different locations. 'Sexuality', as we think of it today, is an invention of the late eighteenth and nineteenth centuries, produced by specific techniques for eliciting confession about individual desires and classifying and interpreting what was disclosed. Such are Foucault's claims in his audacious work on sexuality. This may seem surprising to readers new to Foucault, since commonplace wisdom says that sexuality belongs in the (often held to be unimpeachable) realms of the biological, the genetic, the psychological. We also think of it as something deep-rooted, individual, private and defining; as 'ours'. Sexuality is the ineffable, surely, not a matter of words, constructions and fields of knowledge? This is precisely the kind of thinking with which Foucault wishes to take issue. '[T]his oft-stated theme, that sex is outside of discourse and that only the removing of an obstacle, the breaking of a secret, can clear the way leading to it, is precisely what needs to be examined' (*WK*, p. 34), he claims.

The texts that we know today as Foucault's *History of Sexuality* are a tri-partite collection, the first volume of which, a history of modern sex in the context of a theory of the operations of power and knowledge, was published in France in 1976. Volumes two and three, on ancient conceptions of plea-sure, selfhood and ethics, followed eight years later, in 1984. However, these three books are only a small part of the history of sex that Foucault *intended* to write; and volumes two and three deviated considerably from his original conception of how the completed *History* would look. We know that his plans for this series included projected volumes on the following subjects of mod-ern sexuality: the body and the flesh; children; women, mothers and hysteria; the perverse adult; and populations and races.[1] Instead, as we shall see, he turned to classical sources, and began to undertake a complex investigation of the uses of pleasure and the care of the self in ancient culture. Unfortu-nately, Foucault's death in 1984 prevented the completion of the large-scale modern history, should he have chosen to return to it. The full implications of Foucault's project, then, remain lost to us today. However, the three works that do exist have been enormously influential, particularly volume one, *The Will to Knowledge,* which is often found on university reading lists as an intro-duction to Foucault's thought in general, as well as being recognised as a key text for gay and lesbian studies and for the inaugurators of queer theory (see chapter 7, below). Volumes two and three are significant for offering a prelim-inary sketch of how a Foucaldian ethics of subjectivity might look, and have inspired considerable subsequent critical commentary. The current chapter, then, will offer an introduction to reading the fragments of Foucault's history of sexuality.

The Will to Knowledge

As Beer has analysed impressively in his *Michel Foucault: Form and Power*, the language and rhetoric of *The Will to Knowledge* are particularly complex and rich, and Foucault finds numerous ways to illustrate the styles and movements of the discourses he is historicising and critiquing in his own writing. As is often his preferred method, Foucault begins his text by painting us a picture. Here, it is a rather cartoon-like picture of sexual repression in the European nineteenth century, a picture with which, Foucault says, we should be familiar. Readers of Foucault will know by now that they would do well to be suspicious of anything familiar, any commonplace that they might take for granted. For these are usually the targets of Foucault's analytical and demystifying energies. The case of the 'repressive hypothesis' is no exception. Having presented us with the common features associated with Victorian repressive attitudes towards sex – 'taboo, non-existence and silence' (*WK*, p. 5) – Foucault calls into question the very forms of power and knowledge that the repressive hypothesis pre-supposes. In opposition to the commonly held belief that the Victorian age was characterised by a taboo on speaking about sex, that is, by *prohibition* or the psychoanalytic concept of *repression*, Foucault demonstrates that never before had social subjects so comprehensively been exhorted to produce confessional discourse about their sexual behaviours. This led to the establishment of a set of narratives about unusual and unorthodox practices, to which labels were given, creating a classificatory and disciplinary division between the norm and the 'perverse'. While covering up piano legs, the Victorians were also producing the most extraordinarily detailed statements about their own, and other people's, sex lives. The mistake of history has been to focus on the former phenomenon while ignoring the significance of the latter.

It is proposed that sexuality became a field of scientific knowledge in the late eighteenth and nineteenth centuries, as a result of the waning of the influence of the church in modernity and the concomitant rise of clinic-based sexology and, later, psychoanalysis. Sexology, or *Sexualwissenschaft*, designated a field of inquiry that grew up predominantly in Germany, Austria and France, but that also had representatives throughout Europe in the nineteenth century. It took as its principal object the study of the sexually 'sick', as the title of the most famous bible of sexology, Richard von Krafft-Ebing's *Psychopathia Sexualis* (1886), suggests.[2] Foucault charts the way in which modern sex stopped being simply a matter of acts (sanctioned or sinful) that one carried out, and became instead a means of identifying individuals and groups within the population, via the inscription of sexuality in diagnostic medical discourse. Foucault uses the example – a rather controversial one, perhaps, to the minds of twenty-first-century readers – of the bucolic scene of the 'simple-minded' farmhand (*WK*, p. 31) who liked to obtain caresses from little girls. Where once this would have been considered an innocent event in pastoral life, suddenly policemen, judges and doctors were summoned to produce expert reports and to write this man into a medico-legal narrative. His acts then became a pathologised practice, with a diagnostic label, and the practitioner became a recognisable type of pervert. The purpose of this example is to illustrate that suddenly, in modernity, the knowledge of what someone enjoys doing – their pleasure – is thought to be revelatory of their nature. The paedophile is perhaps the most controversial of all the sexual subjects that the nineteenth century created, from our contemporary viewpoint, but Foucault's example is an effective one in demonstrating that acts which in one historical period are commonly held to be unquestionably immoral, illegal and harmful may, at another time, have been acceptable, common, or have simply passed unnoticed. This is neither a case of moral relativism on Foucault's part nor an ultra-neo-liberal attempt to assert that 'anything goes'; rather it is a reminder, after Nietzsche, that morals themselves have a history – or rather a genealogy – and that these are intimately linked to the types of disciplinary power that operate in a given epoch. The broader implication is that we have *all* been affected by the statements about the truth of sexual identity that the nineteenth century produced. It is through a process of designation or self-designation as a particular sexual identity that we are led to believe that we 'know ourselves', that we have discovered the 'truth' of our being. This belief is revealed by Foucault as a fiction, a myth of origins serving a classificatory and normalising purpose. It is according to this logic that Foucault is able to state that the nineteenth century replaced the sin of sodomy with the 'personage' of the homosexual. The line of continuity between the religious and the scientific operations of power, however, is found in the function of confession. Originally in the Christian confessional, it is now on the psychoanalyst's couch, or in the psychiatrist's clinic, that one enumerates one's unsanctioned acts, desires and even most nebulous fantasies.

Foucault presents a unique view of how official knowledges about sexuality began to infiltrate life in the nineteenth century. Rather like the panoptical power described in *Discipline and Punish*, an all-pervasive regime of sexuality was rigorously asserted: children's bodies and behaviours were scrutinised from all sides, such that 'all around the child, indefinite lines of penetration were disposed' (*WK*, p. 42); the classification of the perversions led to a pluralisation of sexual identities and a 'specification of individuals' (*WK*, pp. 42–3); technologies of health and pathology designed to monitor sexual aberrations gave birth to the pleasures of confessing, resisting, showing off, withholding: an eroticised dance of words that went back and forth between clinician and patient, teacher and pupil, parent and child, and that resulted in 'perpetual spirals of power and pleasure' (*WK*, p. 45). All of these techniques, it is argued, led to a 'sexual saturation' (*WK*, p. 45), totalitarian in its effects, but multiple and infinitely diverse in its means of operation. Foucault's radical and counterintuitive, but beautifully seductive, claim here is that the 'sexual scientists' of the nineteenth century did not invent techniques and methods for *uncovering* the hidden truths about sex; rather they *produced* sexuality as a new category of knowledge, a historically specific field.

It would be too easy, however, to fall into the trap of thinking that sexology and psychoanalysis constituted straightforwardly oppressive forces, or that their taxonomies and diagnoses – the 'medicalization of the sexually peculiar' (*WK*, p. 44) – must be understood as techniques of ethical violence. This thinking is not quite in keeping with the subtle model of power that Foucault is proposing. For him, the making of discursive sex allows also for the subversive possibilities of using the discourse for ends for which it was not intended. By this, we can understand that once a group – for example homosexuals – has been named by sexology, the power of that naming is then available to the 'homosexual' himself, for his own purposes. As well as making it possible to introduce 'social controls into this area of "perversity" [. . .] it also made possible the formation of a "reverse" discourse: homosexuality began to speak on its own behalf, to demand that its legitimacy or "natural" status be acknowledged, often in the same vocabulary, using the same categories by which it was medically disqualified' (*WK*, p. 101).[3] The homosexual, then, could use the medical discourse which spoke of inherited or congenital inversion against the grain of pathology and condemnation, to argue that if this sexual 'preference' were naturally occurring, then it must be as inevitable as heterosexuality, and therefore not a suitable object for punishment. This strategy of reverse discourse allowed for limited emancipatory campaigns using the terms of the medical disciplines themselves. Moreover, the homosexual or pervert, given a label with which to identify, was handed on a plate the means of seeking out like-minded fellows, in order to pursue pleasure, form alliances and create resistant communities using the same name given by the authority discourse, but for very different purposes to the one intended. Thus, we are encouraged to think about the power of discourse in a way that avoids the simplistic binary categories of good/bad, positive/negative. Power is not something that we can reject or accept; it is not avoidable; rather it is everywhere, it constitutes our force field of interaction, the 'lines of penetration' at the point of convergence of which are our bodies and identities. We all have access to it, whether we are using it assertively or reactively, to compel or to resist.

The Will to Knowledge constitutes an admirable illustration of Foucault's assertion that power does not work from the top down – hierarchically or by oppression – but rather from the bottom up, via resistance. Power operates only in a network of power relations, a system in which 'there is no single locus of great Refusal, no soul of revolt, source of all rebellions, or pure law of the revolutionary. Instead there is a plurality of resistances, each of them a special case' (*WK*, pp. 95–6). As we have seen in our discussion of *Discipline and Punish*, this polyvalent model of force and resistance is in stark opposition to earlier theories of power, such as the dyadic model of the Hegelian Master–Slave dialectic or the Marxian critique of class oppression which borrowed from it, in which the proletariat is the 'single locus of great Refusal' and the bourgeoisie the single oppressor.

Similarly, the idea that the compulsion to confess creates the confession, and that the edict to reveal the truth creates the secret itself is at the very heart of Foucault's logic of the discursive nature of power. Thus, claims Foucault, the truth of sex came to be constituted by a *scientia sexualis* in Western Europe, in contrast to the Eastern *ars erotica*. Foucault's characterisation of the Eastern is in some ways, perhaps, naïve, or may even be charged with being a Western projection of the kind Edward Saïd has critiqued in *Orientalism* (1978), in which the white Western subject imagines the East as a continent of mystery and exotic delights – a fantasy which served as implicit justification for colonialism. However, Foucault sets up the East–West binarism here to make a specific point about the operations of discursivity of sex in the West. Foucault claims that in Eastern erotic art, 'truth is drawn from pleasure itself' (*WK*, p. 57) and techniques of bodily pleasure – their intensity and their qualities – are the only features of sex that are sought and refined. This is in contradistinction, Foucault claims, to the Western insistence on finding the underlying motivation for individual sexual behaviour and producing techniques to pathologise and treat the sexually 'sick'. In the light of this analysis, he goes so far as to point out that the process of confession itself began to be productive of a sort of pleasure in modernity, displacing the focus from the pleasures of the body towards the discursive satisfaction felt by a self-confessing subject of knowledge. Foucault is convinced that confession forms the cornerstone of modern sexuality. Language has become saturated with the eroticised pleasure of its own telling. This trend is visible in the history of literature, he claims; his best example of this being Diderot's fable of *Les Bijoux indiscrets* (The Indiscreet Jewels, 1747–8), in which a female sex organ is bewitched and compelled to talk, to tell the stories of the sexual acts it has encountered and the secrets of those with whom it has come into contact. This whimsical tale illustrates for Foucault how 'between each of us and our sex, the West has placed a never-ending demand for truth' (*WK*, p. 77).[4]

As is often the case, Foucault's style itself becomes revelatory of the phenomenon he analyses, such that even *writing about* writing about sex seems inevitably to lead to a vivid lubricity of language. To substantiate this point, Beer gives the example of the reference to 'a kind of generalised discursive erethism' ('une sorte d'éréthisme discursif généralisé') (*WK*, p. 32), a term suggesting a sexual excitation that is linguistic as well as bodily, that stimulates the body via discursive seduction. Similarly, Foucault's keenness to emphasise the multiplication and proliferation of plural discourses about sex is reflected in the many instances of stylistic enumeration in his text: techniques for producing sexuality, disciplines for regulating sexuality, and the types of sexuality produced are described in multi-clausal syntax and in lists. An example of such syntax is seen in the following extract: 'A dissemination, then, of proce-dures of confession, a multiple localization of their constraint, a widening of their domain: a great archive of the pleasures of sex was gradually constituted' (*WK*, p. 63). The function of this style may be twofold: first a ludic illustra-tion of the way in which sexual discourse functions: excitedly tripping over itself in its desire to describe acts and pleasures in the case of literature, or full of classificatory zeal in the case of medical texts. Secondly, however, Foucault may be sounding a warning, alerting us to the fact that he is aware, even in his own text, of the pitfalls of talking about sex. As soon as we engage with the discourse, we are faced with the temptation of trying to prove our own truth position, of becoming a little bit too zealous and enjoying it a bit too much. For even though it critiques what it describes, Foucault's account of the history of sexuality is to some extent, inevitably, also a discourse about sexuality.

Another important function of *The Will to Knowledge* is to develop Fou-cault's Nietzschean ideas on the workings of power. The quasi-Nietzschean title of Foucault's work substitutes knowledge for power, suggesting that the former term functions for Foucault as the latter functions for Nietzsche, as the force fuelling the conflictual (but, paradoxically, productive) struggle of individuals in history. Moreover, the relationship between the articulated term 'knowledge' and the silenced term 'power' is an important one. The two are always close for Foucault, becoming entwined and conjoined around certain cultural/historical sites that constitute particularly potent discursive fields. Fou-cault argues for the political importance of understanding how power really works. He explains the theory of power he is proposing in most detail in a chapter originally entitled 'Dispositifs de la sexualité' and translated by Hurley as 'The Deployment of Sexuality'. I would take issue here with the translation of *dispositif* as 'deployment', since the French does not only connote 'utilisation' or 'mobilisation' (as of troops), but also 'mechanism' or 'strategy', which cor-roborates and expands Foucault's analysis of the pluralisation and dispersal of discourses and the extension of strategic lines of penetration around the objects of sexual study. *Dispositif* also has a juridical meaning, as the operative or enacting part of a judgement, suggesting the precise mechanism by which the operations of sexuality are institutionally put in place.[5] Foucault claims that the power of the monarch and its relation to law is no longer the model of power by which modern societies function. But very few of us understand this: 'at bottom [...] the representation of power has remained under the spell of monarchy In political thought and analysis, we still have not cut off the head of the king' (*WK*, p. 89). Moreover, 'we have been engaged for centuries in a type of society in which the juridical is increasingly incapable of coding power, of serving as its system of representation' (*WK*, p. 89). Foucault argues that, in order properly to understand the workings of power, we must conceive of a model that does not take as its basis the 'theoretical privilege of law and sovereignty' (*WK*, p. 90). To understand the *dispositif* of sexuality in modernity, then, we must cease to think of the powers governing it in terms of negative representation and prohibition, and understand instead that power is mobile, operates from the bottom up rather than repressively from the top down, is 'non-subjective', and always finds resistance in proportion to its exertion. Foucault's vision for rethinking the sexuality–power–knowledge relationship is beautifully summed up in the formula 'sex without the law, and power without the king' (*WK*, p. 91).

The final, and relatively little discussed, chapter of *The Will to Knowledge*, 'Right of Death and Power over Life', identifies the *mode* in which power operates in modernity. The chapter opens with a discussion of ancient sovereign power. The omnipotent right of a monarch to decide over the life and death of his subjects, Foucault claims, was modified by the time theoreticians came to describe it, such that the sovereign could decide only to take the life of one who threatened his own existence and the order of the state. In modernity, rather than power being employed in this defensive way, power is employed proactively and productively. Modern state power is 'bent on generating forces, making them grow, and ordering them' (*WK*, p. 136). Ours is a society in which 'political power has assigned itself the task of administering life' (*WK*, p. 139). The organisation of the population via the regulation and utilisation of its reproductive functions is the form that political power takes in modernity. Foucault terms this sort of organisation 'bio-politics' and the power it wields 'bio-power'. Having established the specificity of bio-politics, he is able to demonstrate why sexuality holds such a special place in the workings of modern power. It was situated, he argues, at the 'pivot of two axes along which developed the entire political technology of life' (*WK*, p. 144). First, it was intimately related to the disciplines of the body described in *Discipline and Punish* and discussed in the previous chapter. Secondly, it was connected to the regulation of the population central to bio-political organisation: 'sex was a means of access both to the life of the body and the life of the species' (*WK*, p. 146).

Rather than being a 'blood' society, characterised by clan-led values of honour, war, glory, the power of the sovereign, etc., we moderns live in a 'sex' society, a culture concerned with the regulation and organisation of the population according to techniques of health care management, discourses regarding population growth, virility and fertility, the attribution to female bodies of maternal functions and roles, etc. Foucault states that 'The new procedures of power that were devised during the classical age and employed in the nineteenth century were what caused our societies to go from *a symbolics of blood to an analytics of sexuality*' (*WK*, p. 148). Having mapped this shift, Foucault makes a characteristic gesture of showing that change is not a matter of absolute separation or total rupture. He refers to the writings of the Marquis de Sade as an illustration of the ways in which the imaginary of blood and that of sex may, in fact, overlap and fuel each other. In the Sadeian universe, the only law is a law of pleasure and pleasure for the sovereign subject is found ultimately in eroticised bloodshed and destruction. Sade's imaginary world thus illustrates the convergence of these regimes.

Foucault states:

> While it is true that the analytics of sexuality and the symbolics of blood were grounded at first in two very distinct regimes of power, in actual fact the passage from one to the other did not come about [. . .] without overlappings, interactions, and echoes. In different ways, the preoccupation with blood and the law has for nearly two centuries haunted the administration of sexuality.
>
> (*WK*, p. 149)

These compelling insights allow Foucault's book to end on an unexpected note, a critique of political ideologies. Foucault describes how in the second half of the nineteenth century 'the thematics of blood', in the form of discourses of race, infiltrated the careful management of sexuality. Foucault is referring here to Degeneration theory, popularised by such scientists as Philippe Buchez in France and Max Nordau, author of *Entartung* (*Degeneration*, 1892), in Germany. Degeneration theory was a *fin-de-siècle* set of pseudo-scientific discourses, which held as a central tenet that the Caucasian races were more 'evolved' than others, and that white Europeans faced accelerated cultural Degeneration as a result of, among other phenomena, racial intermixing.[6] Nazi eugenics had some of its origins in these theories, and it is this that Foucault has firmly in mind when he describes the 'fantasies of blood and the paroxysms of a disciplinary power' (*WK*, p. 149) leading to systematic genocide. Degeneration theory also cited sexual 'inversion' and 'perversion' as both causes and effects of social decline, and sexologists such as Krafft-Ebing, with whom Foucault is concerned in the first half of the book, were themselves to some extent exponents of theories of inherited degenerate traits, such that the critique of eugenics has a specifically sexual flavour. Homosexuals as well as Jews were, after all, the victims of Nazi extermination, as Foucault points out in the interview on cinema, 'Sade: Sergeant of Sex' (1975), to which I have referred in a previous chapter:

The Nazis were charwomen in the bad sense of the term. They worked
with brooms and dusters, wanting to purge society of everything they
considered unsanitary, dusty, filthy; syphilitics, homosexuals, Jews, those
of impure blood, Blacks, the insane. It's the foul *petit bourgeois* dream of
racial hygiene that underlies the Nazi dream. Eros is absent.

(*EW ii*, p. 226)

By invoking Eros, as opposed to the disciplinary systems of sexuality, bodies
and races, at the end of this quotation, Foucault delineates the dangers of a
technology for organising knowledge about sex that can – in extreme historical
circumstances – lead not only to normalisation but also to the elimination of
otherness. As he will write later, as a footnote to this thinking on biopolitics,
'since the population is nothing more than what the state takes care of for
its own sake, of course the state is entitled to slaughter it, if necessary. So the
reverse of biopolitics is thanatopolitics' (*TS*, p. 160).

Foucault's *Will to Knowledge* ends, then, with a specific plea for our analyses
of power and of sexuality: 'We must conceptualise the deployment of sexuality
on the basis of the techniques of power that are contemporary with it' (*WK*,
p. 150). Psychoanalysis, while refusing affiliation with ideas of heredity and
eugenics via Freud's strong rejection of Degeneration theory in the first of
the *Three Essays on the Theory of Sexuality* (1915), nevertheless continued
according to Foucault to behave as if sex was regulated by 'the law, death, blood
and sovereignty' (*WK*, p. 150). This critique of psychoanalysis may be more
particularly applicable to the work of Jacques Lacan than to that of Freud,
though Foucault does not name Lacan here. Lacan's concepts of the Law of the
Father and the operations of the Symbolic Order come closer to articulating
a theory of the Law as the principal force ordering psychical life than Freud's
texts. However, the disruptive powers of the other orders – Imaginary and Real –
in the Lacanian system mean that to consider Lacan's body of work as a totalising
and absolutist theory of psyche governed by Law would be a gross misreading
of his corpus.

Finally, then, Foucault calls in *The Will to Knowledge* for new analyses of the
way in which the sexual field is constructed and strategically used that would
be specific to our own historical context. What is needed, he claims, is an
analysis in which 'the biological and the historical are not consecutive to one
another, as in the evolutionism of the first sociologists, but are bound together
in an increasingly complex fashion in accordance with the development of the
modern technologies of power that take life as their objective' (*WK*, p. 152).
He lays down the gauntlet here for a new critical approach – not to sexuality

itself, but to the questions which are asked about it, and the uses to which it is put, in our own time and place.

Pleasure and the ancient world

The two volumes dealing with ancient sexuality can be read as examples of the classic assertion that Foucault's history is 'a history of the present'. His exploration of the 'Uses of Pleasure' and the 'Care of the Self' constitute analytical histories of Classical antiquity and the early Christian world, but also reflections on the ways in which the concepts of selfhood, relationality and bodily pleasures he uncovers in ancient culture might serve as the basis for an aesthetics and an ethics, or more properly an *askesis* ('an exercise of oneself in the activity of thought', *UP*, p. 9) from which we could learn today, and which might offer a model with which to relativise and modify the structures of sexual knowledge discussed above that would be proper to our historical moment. An ethics of freedom seems to be the aim of Foucault's investigations at this point.

Foucault's introduction to *The Use of Pleasure* constitutes a concise and convincing account of the reasons for the surprising shift from the study of modern sexuality in volume one to the concentration upon ancient sources in volumes two and three. Foucault became convinced that Western culture, in the Christian tradition, has led its subjects to conceive of themselves as 'subjects of desire' (see *UP*, p. 6). By tracing the ancient precursors of modern systems of desire and sexuality in the form of a discontinuous genealogy, Foucault used the ancient past to shed light on the present, directing his study towards 'the practices by which individuals were led to focus their attention on themselves, to decipher, recognise and acknowledge themselves as subjects of desire' (*UP*, p. 5). *The Use of Pleasure* and *The Care of the Self* are, then, in some senses direct pre-histories of *The Will to Knowledge*, since 'in order to understand how the modern individual could experience himself as a subject of a "sexuality", it was essential first to determine how, for centuries, Western man had been brought to recognise himself as a subject of desire' (*UP*, pp. 5–6).

Critics have been divided on the extent to which these two final works mark an abrupt break or about-face in Foucault's thinking, particularly with regard to his long-standing suspicion of the concept of selfhood. The docile bodies of *Discipline and Punish* may be seen to sit uncomfortably alongside the practices of self-stylisation described in these late works. Indeed, Luc Ferry and Alain Renault have asserted that the 'retraction of his later years' is 'profoundly problematical',[7] while Lois McNay has argued conversely that 'practices of the self must be understood as a modification of Foucault's previous intellectual concerns rather than as a refutation of them'.[8] The agency of the subject is certainly seen to be greater here than in studies of the operation of disciplinary power, such as *Discipline and Punish* and *The Will to Knowledge*. However, the subject does not operate *autonomously* but *relatedly*: responding to, rather than in isolation from, social norms. As Foucault comments in 1984, in an interview on 'The ethics of the concern for self as a practice of freedom':

> I would say that if I am now interested in how the subject constitutes himself in an active fashion, by the practices of self, these practices are nevertheless not something invented by the individual himself. They are models that he finds in his culture and are proposed, suggested, imposed upon him by his culture, his society, and his cultural group.
>
> (*EW i*, p. 291)

While looking more closely here at individual agency, Foucault is in no way giving up the idea of a constructed subject in favour of a natural or essential one.

Foucault's methodology in volumes two and three continues to draw on genealogy, but it is also more centrally concerned with 'problematisations'. Foucault seeks to show how in classical antiquity, 'sexual activity and sexual pleasures were problematized through practices of the self, bringing into play the criterion of "an aesthetics of existence"' (*UP*, p. 12). The term 'problematisations', here, then, denotes the means by which individuals confront their existence via a series of choices. The areas of experience which are problematised are culturally specific and determined, but the way in which the individual relates to them and makes creative personal choices within their limits and strictures is what is of interest to Foucault. Problematisations are inherently matters of ethics. We might say that volumes two and three of the *History of Sexuality* constitute a genealogy of the problematisations of sexual life, and supplement historiography with a genuinely inquisitive set of speculations regarding the exercise of freedom within systems of social morality and codes of behaviour (a personal ethics).

A commonly voiced objection to Foucault's project has been the fact that the privileged subjects whose choices and freedoms Foucault focuses on were free male Athenian citizens, not Greeks in general, slaves or women. The possibilities for self-expression and self-stylisation would have been considerably more limited for these marginal subjects. (For more on feminist responses to this aspect of Foucault's work see pp. 104–11 below.) Foucault is clear, however, that the social models he is uncovering in the ancient world should *not* form a utopian template for restructuring our society. Rather, they may offer analogous and heuristic guides for questioning the limits and possibilities of projects of self-creation today.

Foucault examines how, in ancient Greece (for free male citizens), the pleasures of the body were seen as natural. They were also, however, seen as potentially dangerous since they appealed to man's lower or animal side, and because their intensity could lead to overindulgence and thereby to a failure of mastery (*enkrateia*). Because of this, it was necessary for a citizen to discipline himself to enjoy such pleasures judiciously and with measure. Relations with boys were tolerated, and indeed construed as the most exquisite pleasure, but for a citizen to deprive himself of that pleasure demonstrated strength in forgoing (and, incidentally, occasioned the potentially more sublime pleasure of restraint). A certain amount of privation was felt to intensify desire, such that austerity became a means of refining and increasing the pleasure when one finally indulged (*UP*, p. 43). The achievement of self-mastery through the asketic ideal assured for the free Greeks 'a form of wisdom that brought them into direct contact with some superior element in human nature and gave them access to the very essence of truth' (*UP*, p. 20). This, then, is the essence of the Greek understanding of *ethos* (ethics). It is a mode of behaviour in which mastery of the self is both pleasurable and beneficial to self and other. As Foucault summarises in an interview published in 1984:

> *Ethos* was a way of being and of behaviour. It was a way of being for the subject along with a certain way of acting, a way visible to others. A person's *ethos* was visible in his clothing, appearance, gait, in the calm with which he responded to every event and so on. For the Greeks, this was the concrete form of freedom. This was the way they problematized their freedom.
>
> (*EW iii*, p. 286)

Notwithstanding the perceived benefits of austerity, many free citizens in Greek culture, however, enjoyed a full range of bodily pleasures – with men, with women, inside and outside of marriage. Austerity was not an authoritarian imposition, a requirement, but a 'supplement' or a guide to good living.

Moreover, unlike in the modern scientific sexual imaginary that Foucault analysed in *The Will to Knowledge*, in ancient culture men were not categorised according to which bodily practices they preferred, or with whom they preferred to carry them out. Classifications existed, but men were differentiated from each other according to the intensity of their pleasures, and their degree of activity or passivity within sexual practice. Immorality (in the form of lack of mastery) was attributed equally to the man whose sexual behaviour was excessive or uncontrolled, and to the man who played the passive role in sex, a role 'properly' designated to women, boys and slaves (*UP*, p. 47).

Foucault initially finds that there appear to have been fewer differences between ancient Greek culture and early Christianity than we might think. Both expressed reservations about the effects of unbridled indulgence in sexual pleasure and both – in principle at least – prized fidelity in marriage. The moral structures governing life differed very little, with some exceptions such as a diminution of tolerance of same-sex relationships within Christianity. But where the subtle, but significant, difference lies is in the degree of liberty accorded to the subject with regard to his freedom to interpret the rules of his society and adapt his own behaviour to it. For along with the incitement to moderation, the Greek citizen was encouraged to engage in a project of concern for the self that involved a much greater degree of flexibility and freedom than the Christian subject enjoyed. Foucault is careful to assert that, for the Greeks, 'themes of sexual austerity should be understood, not as an expression of, or commentary on, deep and essential prohibitions, but as the elaboration and stylisation of an activity in the exercise of its power and the practice of its liberty' (*UP*, p. 23).

In the Christian worldview, bodily pleasures were no longer seen as natural and inevitable joys to be used sparingly and artfully, but as temptations to sin, and so a matter for prohibition and absolute abstention. Whereas in the ancient Greek world, *ta aphrodisia* were an important part of life which simply had to be managed responsibly, in Christianity they were absolutely prohibited other than within marriage, for procreative aims. Foucault distinguishes between moral systems in which 'code' is more important than 'ethics' and vice versa. He sees Christianity as a system of morality in which codes are more important than ethics, insofar as individuals are called upon to obey absolutely the externally imposed rules of behaviour, rather than to interpret and modify cultural codes in the service of a personal ethics. The externalisation of conflict within Christianity, in which temptation comes from Satan and redemption is given by God, led to the subject seeking an understanding of the self only in order to renounce mastery (in the classical sense of self-control and moderation) and turn the self, devoid of passions, over to the will of God.

Foucault relates this shift to a break in the history of the conceptualisation of 'care for the self' (*epimeleia heautou*). He argues that where once the cultivation of self was perceived as a fundamental aspect of civic good conduct in the search for an ethics of pleasure, later, under the Roman Empire and the Christian religion, the self became an object of knowledge and interrogation, and the aim of this interrogation greater purification. The body capable of experiencing pleasure was increasingly the object of suspicion, as pleasure was felt to lead to weakness and ill health. Whereas in Classical morals men were expected to be (more or less) faithful to their wives, not out of respect for an equal but in order to demonstrate the 'elegant' sexual continence of which a superior citizen was capable, in Graeco-Roman culture the reciprocal bond of marriage leading to reproduction was insisted upon, and sexual behaviour became increasingly austere. Foucault argues that the strengthening of the marriage bond led to a disinvestment from relationships with boys, and from same-sex pleasures in general:

> Thus there begins to develop an erotics different from the one that had taken its starting point in the love of boys, even though abstention in sexual pleasures plays an important part in both. This new erotics organises itself around the symmetrical and reciprocal relationship of a man and a woman, around the high value attributed to virginity, and around the complete union in which it finds perfection.
>
> (*CS*, p. 232)

Abstention from sex with boys thus became a matter of obedience to law, rather than a matter of individual self-mastery leading to a Platonic spiritual 'high'.

Although the discourse of absolute sin and evil did not make itself manifest until Christianity was firmly established, Foucault's third volume charts how in the time of the Roman Empire, a line was crossed between austerity as a practice of individual freedom, and obedience to a prescriptive code of moral conduct – 'an experience in which the relation to self takes the form not only of a domination but also of an enjoyment without desire and without disturbance' (*CS*, p. 68). Foucault goes on:

> One is still far from an experience of sexual pleasure where the latter will be associated with evil, where behaviour will have to submit to the universal form of law, where the deciphering of desire will be a necessary condition for acceding to a purified existence. Yet one can already see how the question of evil begins to work upon the ancient theme of force, how the question of law begins to modify the theme of art and *techné*, and how the question of truth and the principle of self-knowledge evolve within the ascetic practices.
>
> (*CS*, p. 68)

Foucault concludes his history of ancient sexuality with a summary of the evolution of the problematic of *assujettissement* from one system to another: 'the code elements that concern the economy of pleasures, conjugal fidelity and relations between men may well remain analogous, but they will derive from a profoundly altered ethics and from a different way of constituting oneself as the ethical subject of one's sexual behaviour' (*CS*, p. 240). There is a profound difference, Foucault thinks, between a system in which one understands the moral codes of one's culture and yet is free to adapt them creatively to one's own conduct, and a system in which an externally imposed series of moral rules governs the individual's conduct through that individual's fear of retribution. In the latter system, renunciation, rather than cultivation, of the self is the result.

Ethics, Eros and freedom

The writing on the 'care of the self' marked the first step in an unfinished project, related to, but separate from, the ongoing *History of Sexuality*, and likewise interrupted by death. In a lecture he gave at the University of Vermont in 1982, entitled 'Technologies of the Self', Foucault announced his interest in 'a genealogy of how the subject constituted *itself* as subject' (*TS*, p. 4). This would be an ethical inquiry into 'the freedom of people' that would counter the traditional ethics of humanism with a *ethos* closer to the Greek care for the self: 'What I am afraid of about humanism is that it presents a certain form of our ethics as a universal model for any kind of freedom. I think that there are more secrets, more possible freedoms, and more inventions in our future than we can imagine in humanism' (*TS*, p. 15). Foucault identifies this ethical suspicion of universal humanism as one of the concerns underlying his entire corpus. It was via the lures of humanism, he claims that 'we' constituted ourselves as subjects through the exclusion of others: the insane, the criminal, the perverted. Foucault wonders if there would be a form of ethics of the self that would not work to construct and 'other' certain subjects as 'the abnormal', and that would be compatible with a mode of democratic political life.

In an interview in 1984, Foucault revisited his position on liberation – a concept with which, as we have seen, he had had generally very little sympathy – and conceded that 'liberation is sometimes the political or historical condition for a practice of freedom' (*EW iii*, p. 283). However, Foucault asserts that this liberation is not a pathway to inevitable human happiness, and 'freedom' is not absolute or divorced from the influence of other plays of force and will. Liberation, rather, 'paves the way for new power relationships, which must be controlled by practices of freedom' (*EW iii*, pp. 283–4). 'Practices of freedom' here, understood both in regard to, and outside of, the context of sexuality, seem to suggest the mechanism of mobility. Foucault seems to suggest that there will always be relationships of power, inside and outside of institutional systems, but they need not always take the form of sclerotic, disciplinary power that reifies hierarchy. An ethics of freedom would keep power relations between the individual and the state in a condition of flux and play. It is only via non-disciplinary freedom, argues Foucault, that 'ethics' can have any meaning; 'for what is ethics if not [. . .] the conscious practice of freedom. [. . .] Freedom is the ontological condition of ethics' (*EW iii*, p. 284).

Foucault has more to say here about power relationships, freedom and ethics, and offers some concrete examples of the distinction between the operation of provisional power and the exercise of force via the exploitation of hierarchy, which are worth quoting at length:

> Power is not evil. Power is games of strategy. [. . .] For example, let us take sexual or amorous relationships: to wield power over the other in a sort of open-ended strategic game where the situation may be reversed is not evil; it's a part of love, of passion, of sexual pleasure. And let us take as another example [. . .] the pedagogical institution. I see nothing wrong in the practice of a person who, knowing more than others in a specific game of truth, tells those others what to do, teaches them, and transmits knowledge and techniques to them. The problem in such practices where power – which is not a bad thing – must inevitably come into play is knowing how to avoid the kind of domination effects where a kid is subjected to the arbitrary and unnecessary authority of a teacher or a student put under the thumb of a professor who abuses his authority. I believe that this problem must be framed in terms of rules of law, rational techniques of government and *ethos*, practices of the self and of freedom.
>
> (*EW iii*, pp. 298–9)

It is here that the ethics of the self come into play again. The game of power relations can only operate ethically if the subjects in the game both have access to freedom and both operate *ethos* in the way that Foucault understands it here, borrowing from the Greek notion (but abstracting from the context of Greek culture with its citizens, slaves and women). Only when one respects an ethics of self, Foucault argues, can one engage responsibly in the inevitable power games of political and civic life without hierarchy giving rise to domination or oppression.

Foucault's ethics is clearly, as John Rajchman has explored in his book, an *ethos* of Eros.[9] He means this both in so far as amorous relations and bonds are central to Foucault's way of imagining ethical possibilities, and because Foucault's ethical writing, in its curiosity and passion, 're-eroticised the activity of philosophical or critical thought for our times'.[10] In sketching his history of the ways in which subjects are taught to conceptualise themselves as 'subjects of desire', and in looking for pockets of ethical resistance to the disciplining of sexual subjects via 'technologies of the self', Foucault's *History of Sexuality*, and his reflections about the processes of writing it, did important groundwork for those late-twentieth and early twenty-first-century academic and political fields of inquiry concerned explicitly with interrogating the truth of sexual knowledge, as I shall explore in the next chapter.

Chapter 7

Critical receptions

> Sexuality is something that we ourselves create – it is our own creation, and much more than the discovery of a secret side of our desire. We have to understand that with our desires, through our desires, go new forms of relationships, new forms of love, new forms of creation. Sex is not a fatality: it's a possibility for creative life.
>
> Michel Foucault

In this final chapter, I shall explore some of the afterlives of Foucault's work, in particular by charting and evaluating the influence of his ideas about the body, pleasure, power and discourse for academic theory and political praxis, in the forms of feminism, gender studies, gay and lesbian studies and queer theory.

Foucault and feminism

Foucault's work has a contentious and problematic status for feminist theorists, and the reception of his work in this context has been very mixed. Few feminists working within the French philosophical tradition over the past twenty years have used his work to any extent, as the disciplinary bent of influential French thinkers such as Luce Irigaray and Julia Kristeva is largely psychoanalytic. Moreover, while both these feminist theorists have critiqued discourse, they have tended to assume that Western discourse is univocally masculine and phallocentric, in contradistinction to Foucault's view of discourse – and the power which attaches to it – as ambiguous, elastic and plurivocal, capable of being used against dominant trends, of offering counterattack. In an Irigarayan model, women must invent their own ways of speaking and gesturing, outside of masculine logical models. In a Foucaldian perspective, neither men *nor* women have total control over discourse.[1] It is, therefore, mainly among Anglo-American feminists with a sociological affiliation, rather than in his own country, that Foucault's work has been addressed and partially taken up by and for feminism.

A masculine bias is often attributed to Foucault's work by readers such as Sandra Lee Bartky, who, in 1988, made the criticism that, although Foucault is interested in the processes by which disenfranchised subjects are constructed – an agenda shared by feminism – the subjects of Foucault's inquiries (the insane, the criminal, the male homosexual) are, almost without exception, masculine.[2] It is a pity that Foucault's untimely demise prevented the writing of the volume of the *History of Sexuality* devoted to women, maternity and hysteria, as it might have offered a more focused insight into his use of a genealogical method for feminist inquiry. Bartky also makes the critique that, as his corpus stands, little specific attention is paid by Foucault to the particular means by which female 'docile bodies' are created, or the ways in which women may resist or reverse the operations of discursive power which construct their social roles. One exception to Foucault's alleged androcentrism is his short co-authored text, published in the *Nouvel Observateur* in November 1973, in which he discusses pro-abortion legislation, a social issue about which he campaigned as part of the Groupe d'Information sur la santé (a patients' rights group) alongside feminists, to promote 'abortion, contraception and the free use of one's body as rights' (*EW iii*, 425). As we have seen previously, the focus of Foucault's strictly theoretical concerns and his personal political activism are often not self-identical, and it is significant that he was prepared to take civic action regarding an issue pertaining to women which he may not have *theorised* fully.

It is in exploring their underlying, rather than explicit, methodological and political agendas that a *rapprochement* between feminism and Foucault's theory must be attempted. An obvious point of similarity between Foucaldian and feminist thought is the mistrust and critique of the political value of revolution or liberationist agendas. The so-called sexual revolution of the 1960s is a key example. As Jana Sawicki puts it: 'Foucault and feminists both challenged the sexual liberationism of the sixties for similar reasons. Both recognised that power relations governing sexuality run deeper than is presupposed by strategies that simply aim to lift restrictions on sexual behaviour.'[3] Their shared suspicion of the promise of liberation, then, potentially unites Foucault and feminists in a truly critical project.

Irene Diamond and Lee Quinby, in the introduction to their volume on Foucault and feminism, focus on the possibilities of just such dialogue or 'friendship' between feminism and Foucaldian thought: that is, a non-hierarchical relation of interaction between the feminist concern for female subjectivity and Foucault's position with regard to male homosexuality which might suggest new political strategies.[4] This political or discursive strategy, however, is not one that Foucault himself ever articulated. Indeed, Foucault expressed in 1981, in an interview on the subject of 'monosexualism' or living in single-sex communities, relatively little enthusiasm for, or interest in, the possibility of gay male–feminist alliances. He states: 'the promise that we would love women as soon as we were no longer condemned for being gay was utopian. And utopian in the dangerous sense, not because it promised good relations with women, but because it was at the expense of monosexual relations' (*EW i*, p. 161). Foucault was more interested in single-sex male communitarian possibilities, then, than in allying a post-homophobic politics with a feminist agenda; a position with which lesbian separatist feminist politics would have had no problem, but which bespeaks little solidarity with a less radical feminism interested in a politics of co-operation or 'friendship'.

Diamond and Quinby point out a further central tension between Foucaldian thought and much feminist praxis: their attitudes towards subjectivity. While Foucault takes pains to illustrate how the subject with a knowable identity is the effect of the operations of regimes of truth – Foucaldian *assujettissment* – feminism has tended to take the female subject as a given, as the foundation of its politics. In this, feminism may inadvertently 'contribute to, rather than resist, normalising power'.[5] Diamond and Quinby's argument is that where feminism can borrow most profitably from Foucault is in paying attention to his suspicion of subjectivity and his analyses of the ways in which subjects are produced, in order to question essentialist assumptions about the feminine. Where often feminism has questioned the *terms* of how femininity has been defined (whether the model of femininity proposed by dominant discourse is accurate/ appropriate/ empowering), a post-Foucaldian feminism might reject the assumption of the category of 'women' itself as having any valid truth status. As John Rajchman has put it, a Foucaldian modern ethics 'instead of attempting to determine what we should do on the basis of what we essentially are, attempts by analysing who we have been constituted to be, to ask what we might become'.[6] This suggests a particularly apt agenda for a twenty-first-century feminist politics.

However, as Foucault's theory of individual ethics is based on his late work inspired by the figure of the free Greek male (even though Foucault is explicit that this ancient subject must not be taken as a *model* for a modern ethics), it is itself a problematic source of political inspiration for feminists. Joan Grimshaw has argued that 'there are some obvious – and some less obvious – reasons why the ethic of care for the self in antiquity [. . .] seems light-years from anything that any feminist might want to endorse'.[7] The most obvious reason is perhaps the elitism as well as the masculinism of the political context defining it. More fundamentally, however, Grimshaw goes on to argue that what, in earlier Foucault, constituted the effects of 'discipline' – internalised processes of self-surveillance and self-regulation – is suddenly, in later Foucault, taken to constitute a practice of self-stylising ethics and the conduit to freedom. She is unconvinced by the neat division between that which we perform unquestioningly, because we have internalised the codes of our culture, and that which we choose for ourselves as a model of ethical living predicated on measure and self-control. She takes her objection further to argue that many of the 'asketic' practices of self-control we can observe today are heavily, if implicitly, gendered, with dieting, cosmetic surgery, and other modes of beautification being exemplary modern *feminine* practices in which it is difficult to separate the idea of a self-policing conformity to a norm from the deployment of techniques of creative self-stylisation or self-expression.[8] Grimshaw argues that late Foucault is ultimately disappointing in failing to address numerous blind spots in his discourse of freedom – namely race and class, as well as gender. He ignores the work already done by Anglo-American feminists in problematising such issues as consent and freedom within a social context, and thereby risks undermining his own earlier work (especially *Discipline and Punish* and *The Will to Knowledge*) which had critiqued so sensitively the specificities of the disciplinary operations of power and knowledge.

Conversely, it is Foucault's late work on the fashioning of the self that Lois McNay takes as the most fruitful starting point for developing the use of Foucault for feminism, precisely because 'Foucault's work on the ethics of self resonates with some of the essentializing assumptions that underlie radical feminist work on "feminine" or "mothering" ethics'[9] and because '[Foucault's] emphasis on the constitutive powers of discourse reminds feminists that the problem of feminine identity is better approached as an historically and culturally specific construct rather than as an innate phenomenon'.[10] McNay's careful analysis shows how Foucault's later model of subjectivity, operating as an interaction or negotiation between overarching social codes and individual practices of ethics, can be useful for a nuanced account of the position of different groups of women in contemporary culture (single women, mothers, socio-economically privileged women, ethnic minority women). What Grimshaw critiques as a lack in late Foucault is precisely what McNay takes as an inspiration to go several steps further than Foucault in theorising the relation between choice, freedom and cultural codes, particularly with regard to ethnicity.

If Foucault continues to pose a problem for heterosexual feminists, what is the extent of his influence and potential value for a lesbian ethics or politics?

On the subject of female homosexuality/homosociality also, Foucault made statements that can, if read in a certain way, be considered politically troubling for a lesbian readership. In an interview on 'Friendship as a Way of Life' he comments on the publication of Lillian Faderman's book *Surpassing the Love of Men*. On the subject of love between women, and borrowing from Faderman, Foucault states:

> The book shows the extent to which woman's body has played a great role and the importance of physical contact between women: women do each other's hair, help each other with make up, dress each other. Women have had access to the bodies of other women: they put their arms around each other, kiss each other. Man's body has been forbidden to other men in a much more drastic way.
>
> (*EW i*, pp. 138–9)

On the one hand, this suggestion is very close to the spirit of the work of lesbian feminist Adrienne Rich on the 'lesbian continuum'.[11] Rich argues that the history of subtle and covert alliances between women in loving – not always explicitly eroticised – relationships within and despite patriarchy constitutes a silenced history of female homosocial solidarity. The lesbian continuum exists, and is a source of pleasure and power, precisely because men do not perceive female friendships as politically potent or dangerous. It is also the case, however, that other lesbian feminists may take issue with Foucault's statement because, although it takes account of the way in which the lesbian continuum can operate within, and as the blind spot of, patriarchy, it does not offer any strategy of resistance whereby those power structures may be changed, or problematise adequately the fact that no full lesbian subject is allowed for in this formulation. If we wish to remain true to the spirit of Foucault's political position, this lack of legitimate subjectivity will not pose too much of a problem, given that Foucault is consistent in arguing for the power of resistance (that is, the power to be found in voicing dissent – reverse discourse – from an apparently marginal or inferior subject *position* rather than from a locus of subjectivity), and would reject the notion of 'patriarchy' as a monolithic oppressive institution. This obviates the objections of a more straightforward or 'commonsensical' concept of both power and subjectivity. However, it remains the case that Foucault has much to say about the models of social life and political practice that male homosexuality can offer, and almost nothing to say about friendship between women or lesbian feminism, beyond his limited comments on Faderman's book.

One lesbian feminist who has found Foucault useful for theorising her own position and pleasures, however, is Ladelle McWhorter, whose unusual book, *Bodies and Pleasures: Foucault and the Politics of Sexual Normalization*, takes the form of a confessional, semi-autobiographical work, in which McWhorter reads Foucault through the lens of her personal experience as a woman who desires other women and who, ever since childhood, has felt aware of the weight of normalising discourses and surprised and dismayed by the fact that this preference should make her into 'any [particular] kind of person'.[12] The book is unusual in so far as it uses confessional discourse about sexuality – the target of Foucaldian critique in *The Will to Knowledge* – but in such a way as to illustrate the strength of Foucault's argument concerning the ubiquity of discourses of 'truth' surrounding sexual identity:

> For a while, although I persisted in my homosexual behavior, I refused to assume an identity that would consume me and erase all I took myself to be. I resisted the imperative to be a homosexual. But I failed. The very project of resisting this essentializing and totalizing categorization of me propelled me into it. In order to protect myself from serious harm – from losing my sense of myself by being reduced to my sexuality, I had to make my sexuality into a central category, a central issue in my life; I had to allow my sexuality and the epistemic demands surrounding it to pervade (as a rigidly policed silence) everything I said and did.[13]

The book constitutes an interesting example of the strength of Foucault's writing to affect the political strategies of individual readers. It is also a bizarre and challenging application of Foucault in the service of sexual and academic autobiography, a confessional mode which Foucault himself would surely have held in suspicion, but which serves here, as the above quotation makes clear, to affirm the potency of the discourse of 'sexual identity' and the field of power in which it operates – an extremely Foucaldian point.

Feminism's long-debated 'problem' with regard to Foucault, as we have seen, rests largely on the question of whether feminists are interested in reformulating the concepts of power and identity, such that the notions of a stable female subject position and a homogeneous, oppressive field of patriarchy might be radically called into question. Given strands of feminist thought and individual thinkers committed to such projects, such as Sawicki and McNay, can find a fruitful ally in Foucault. Those who view feminism largely as an identity politics based on the stable notion of woman as central common denominator may feel frustrated by Foucault's dual gesture of exhorting us to be suspicious of identity categories while simultaneously pursuing an interest in gay male 'monosexualism' (wanting to have it both ways, some might say). Despite the troubled relationship between Foucault and feminism, then, the Anglo-American academy has made intermittent use of his work for its development of post-structuralist and post-modernist feminist theory. Recent works by authors discussed above have examined the possibilities of fruitful applications of Foucaldian genealogical critique to the conditions of production of the category of 'woman' and 'lesbian', and have staged productive dialogues between Foucault and feminisms.

Foucault and queer theory

The principal way in which Foucault's thought has been used for the growing field of interdisciplinary sexuality studies is via the exploitation of his history and analyses of discourses of knowledge as an alternative to attempts to discover truths about the nature of sexuality. He effectively shifts the focus of the lens so that it no longer points at sexual behaviour but at the discourses that describe it. In particular, Foucault's strategies provide an alternative to the demand for an answer to the question that has for many years dominated the social and medical sciences' explorations and theorisations of sexuality: is homosexuality (or bisexuality, or perversion, or female passivity/male activity etc.) 'innate' or 'acquired'? Are these supposed phenomena biological givens or social constructs? In response to an interviewer asking Foucault whether he had an opinion on the acquired or innate status of homosexuality, Foucault categorically stated: 'On this question I have absolutely nothing to say. "No comment"' (*EW i*, p. 142).

Despite his (strategic) lack of interest in the question, Foucault's work has broadly contributed to those theories that problematise the 'natural' status of sexuality and posit gender, sex and sexuality as social and historically contingent, rather than as natural categories. Mary McIntosh argued in 1968, several years before the first publication of *The Will to Knowledge*, for a social constructionist perspective on homosexuality, drawing on comparative anthropological accounts and considering homosexuality primarily as a 'social category rather than a medical or psychiatric one'.[14] Scholars who attribute the birth of constructionist sexuality studies to the reception of Foucault, then, may be doing a disservice to earlier writers. However, one cannot overstate the extent to which Foucault's ideas in *The Will to Knowledge* were key to the development of constructionist theories of sexuality and gender in the late twentieth century. 'Constructionist' approaches are characterised by a suspicion of purely biological explanations of sex and gender, and of any assumption that a 'natural' sex or sexuality exists. At the very end of *The Will to Knowledge*, Foucault announces this agenda implicitly. His book, he states, has set out to show 'how deployments [*dispositifs*] of power are directly connected to the body – to bodies, functions, physiological processes, sensations, and pleasures' (*WK*, pp. 151–2).

Forms of power and ideology construct specific kinds of pleasures and bodies, states Foucault, and it is wrongheaded to assume the converse: that historically observable manifestations of sexuality, gender and the body follow on naturally or neutrally from purely biological realities.

The most extreme contemporary exponent of such theories is probably the American philosopher Judith Butler, author of *Gender Trouble: Feminism and the Subversion of Identity* (1990) and *Bodies that Matter* (1993). In the former work, Butler argues for the denaturalisation of gender identity categories which, she argues, are a political fiction. By repetitively and unconsciously *performing* the gender ascribed to our sex, we make it appear as a naturally occurring reality. Only by self-consciously playing with gender – through politicised drag – can we disrupt the fiction.[15] In *Bodies that Matter*, Butler argues that not only gender and sexuality, but also bodies, are constructed according to normative binary thinking, that excludes, others or causes to disappear those bodies that fail to conform to social expectations: the bodies that don't signify or 'matter' in the hetero-normative, binary-gendered system according to which our culture operates. Intersexed bodies (in earlier decades called 'hermaphrodites') exemplify these bodies that do not 'matter'. Foucault's interest in similar questions is seen in his presentation of the memoirs of Herculine Barbin, a nineteenth-century hermaphrodite, raised as a girl, but in adulthood – after undergoing medical examinations that pronounced her more properly 'male' – forced to adapt instead to living as a man (*HB*). This case study represents an attempt to explore the life history of a subject whose body does not conform to societal expectations. The case has remarkable resonances with a twentieth-century instance of sexological interference in gender and sexed identity, that of the infamous 'John/Joan' case in the USA in the 1970s, which Butler discusses in detail in her recent book, *Undoing Gender* (2004). When David Reimer suffered an accident as a baby that resulted in the complete loss of his penis, sexologist John Money persuaded his parents to raise him as a girl, 'Joan', using a combination of hormone therapy, the encouraging of 'appropriate' gender-role behaviour and sexological treatment with Money himself. In adulthood, 'Joan' felt unhappy with 'her' identity and underwent gender reassignment treatment to 'become' a man. However, even after the sex reassignment surgery his depression persisted, resulting in suicide in 2004. Both Herculine Barbin and David Reimer committed suicide after the pressure to conform to a medical norm of both societal gender and physiological sex became intolerable. It is in the light of such case studies that the very real political weight of Foucault's and Butler's work on identity becomes most visible.

Whereas Butler has developed nascent ideas in Foucault's work which suggest that sex, sexuality and gender are not naturally occurring but discursively constructed categories, Eve Kosofsky Sedgwick has built on Foucault's interest in the relationship of knowledge to power, and the assertion that sexuality is not only constructed as a secret to be confessed, but as *the secret* of modernity. Her *Epistemology of the Closet* demonstrates how Western discourse from the end of the nineteenth century organises all knowledge according to binary divisions that can, to greater or lesser degrees, be explicitly mapped on to the homosexual/heterosexual distinction: '*Epistemology of the Closet* proposes that many of the major nodes of thought and knowledge in twentieth-century Western culture as a whole are structured – indeed, fractured, by a chronic, now endemic crisis of homo/heterosexual definition, indicatively male, dating from the end of the nineteenth century.'[16] Sedgwick's striking argument is that, owing to the pervasive power of the field of 'sexuality' as defined by Foucault, all Western thought must be analysed in the light of our understanding of its workings.

She also forcefully demonstrates Foucault's assertion that sexual truth is the secret which constantly demands to be told, by showing that silence – staying closeted – may be as meaningful and as performative as any act of verbal coming out; that 'ignorance is as potent and as multiple a thing [...] as is knowledge'.[17] Sedgwick demonstrates the counterintuitive notion – distilled from Foucault's alternative model of power – that positive knowledge is not identical with power. Sometimes, ignorance can 'collude or compete with knowledge in mobilizing the flows of energy, desire, goods, meanings, persons'.[18] Sedgwick's example of this is of two politicians in dialogue, one of whom speaks only his own language. Through his ignorance, the monoglot has the advantage of being able to negotiate in his native tongue while his more learned and knowledgeable polyglot colleague must shoulder the extra burden of setting out his stall in a second or third language.

Butler's and Sedgwick's post-Foucaldian texts form the cornerstone of Anglo-American academic queer theory. So what, then, is 'queer'? One of the principal achievements of queer, of which Foucault would no doubt have been proud, is its systematic rejection of limiting identity categories in favour of a problematisation of the assumption that truth lies in identity. In tandem with this calling into question of identity goes an analysis of the rhetorical means by which these truth claims operate in the political sphere. In an interview in 1982, Foucault opined: 'the relationships we have to have with ourselves are not ones of identity, rather they must be relationships of creation, of innovation. To be the same is really boring. We must not exclude identity if people find their pleasure through this identity, but we must not think of this identity as an ethical universal rule' (*EW i*, p. 166). Elsewhere, Foucault writes: 'another thing to distrust is the tendency to relate the question of homosexuality to the problem of "Who am I?" and "What is the secret of my desire?"' (*EW i*,

p. 135).[19] Queer, then, responds directly to Foucault's challenges regarding the dangers of the complacency of identity. Alexander Doty, author of the beautifully named *Making Things Perfectly Queer*, defines the aim of queer as being to 'challenge or transgress established straight *or gay and lesbian* understandings of gender and sexuality'.[20] And, as Judith Butler puts it, neatly upending the notion that the knowledge of how we look, what we do in bed, and with whom we do it is enough to indicate an essential, meaningful and predictably sewn-together identity: 'there are no direct expressive or causal links between sex, gender, gender presentation, sexual practice, fantasy and sexuality. None of these terms captures or determines the rest.'[21] Queer, then, resists the certainties of knowledge as an intrinsic part of its discursive force.

However, it is important to acknowledge that queer, while rejecting the fixed binary labels problematised by Sedgwick, has a history in identity politics, and that it developed directly from gay and lesbian liberation discourses at a given cultural moment, as a result of a strategic public response to certain cultural, medical and political events. In the 1980s, the decade of Foucault's death from a HIV-related illness, the proliferation of media and medical discourses of AIDS as a 'gay disease' and the homophobic climate to which this both bore witness and contributed gave rise to a situation in which activists grouped together to protest against the stereotyping of, and prejudice against, gay-identified males in such spheres as public health policy-making, sex education and insurance provision. The proliferation of medical and social discourses around GRIDS ('gay-related immune deficiency syndrome', later renamed AIDS, 'acquired' replacing 'gay-related') illustrated in exemplary fashion Foucault's assertions regarding the dangers of a system of knowledge based on identity labels. The act of promiscuous penetrative anal sex without a condom and the identity 'gay man' were collapsed unquestioningly on to each other, with disastrous consequences for gay-identified males with all types of preferences and practices. The label 'queer', traditionally a derogatory homophobic insult, was taken up as the badge of Queer Nation, which developed in New York City in the summer of 1990 and borrowed the direct action tactics of ACT UP. According to Stephen Engel it 'attempted to overcome internal division within the movement and set forth a new seemingly post-identity-based agenda in which all elements of the gay, lesbian, bisexual and transgender community could come together under a single unifying banner'.[22] The actions of these groups, according to David Halperin, represented a truly Foucaldian political strategy, exemplifying the triumph of reverse discourse – a communal act of resistance to, and subverting of, authority discourses, rather than a grand revolutionary gesture.[23] In short, queer was born out of identity politics, at a moment when the danger of politically identifying oneself as gay was most pronounced. Queer, then, came about in a very Foucaldian sense, as the response of the gay movement to the institutionalisation of knowledge about the 'gay disease', and that made its political attack at the level of discourse, responding, countering and twisting the accusatory label 'queer' so that it began to mean *something else*. No longer a self-loathing nomenclature, or a quest for liberation based solely on fixed notions of 'identity', queer instead became a play with knowledge production: a means of resisting homophobia which exposed the mechanisms of oppression rather than arguing for 'rights' within the terms of the dominant culture.

The plural critique of discourses of gender, sex, sexuality, healthy and harmful practices, and identities that arose in the context of the queer backlash against AIDS discourses has produced a strategic radical tool with which to problematise *all* normative discourses about sexual preferences, practices and relationship structures. As Tamsin Spargo explains in her useful little book, *Foucault and Queer Theory*:

> [A]s Foucault's history had shown, [...] object choice had not always constituted the basis for an identity and, as many dissenting voices suggested, it was not inevitably the crucial factor in everyone's perception of their sexuality. This model effectively made bisexuals seem to have a less secure or developed identity (rather as essentialist models of gender make transsexuals incomplete subjects), and excluded groups that defined their sexuality through activities and pleasures rather than gender preferences, such as sadomasochists.[24]

Although he occasionally identified with the label 'homosexual' or 'gay' for local, strategic political reasons, it was 'activities and pleasures', such as the ones found in sadomasochism, rather than the identity labels given by the medical disciplines, that interested Foucault the most in his discussions of the ethical and political potential of the erotic. In dialogues and interviews conducted in the 1980s, Foucault gestured towards an agenda for transgressing the discursive traps of sexuality and subjectivity he had identified in *The Will to Knowledge*, when writing: 'The rallying point for the counterattack against the deployment of sexuality ought not to be sex-desire, but bodies and pleasures' (*WK*, p. 157). Taking the gay SM subcultures of 1980s San Francisco as his inspiration, Foucault argued that it is by engaging in activities and desiring dynamics which avoid aping heterosexuality and socially approved coupledom that dissident pleasure may be experienced separately from normative discourse. With its conscious and playful mimicking of power structures, sadomasochism was seen by Foucault as a particularly rich source of subversion. The sadomasochistic ghettos were held up as paradigmatic alternative communities because they escaped regulatory cultural mechanisms by organising themselves around principles of pleasure and playfulness. Such communities do not contribute to the social order, but parallel and parody it, refusing the utilitarian applications to which 'sexuality' is habitually put. Foucault claims: 'S&M is the eroticization of power, the eroticization of strategic relations. What strikes me with regard to S&M is how it differs from social power. What characterizes power is that it is a strategic relation which has been stabilised through institutions' (*EW i*, p. 169).

Similarly, Foucault argues, the potential within gay SM scenes for reversing power roles and for being alternately 'active' and 'passive' may help to undo the conventional associations of masculinity with domination and empowerment on which heteronormative culture rests:

> Even the Greeks had a problem with being the passive partner in a love relationship. For a Greek nobleman to make love to a passive male slave was natural, since the slave was by nature an inferior; but when two Greek men of the same social class made love it was a real problem because neither felt he should humble himself before the other.
>
> Today homosexuals still have this problem. Most homosexuals feel that the passive role is in some way demeaning. S&M has actually helped alleviate this problem somewhat.
>
> (*EW i*, p. 152)

Gay SM, suggests Foucault, may help men to 'unlearn' the rules of patriarchy (though he probably wouldn't have used the term 'patriarchy'). Queer thinkers post-Foucault, interested in the potential of undoing received ideas about the nature of male and female bodily desires and identities, have taken Foucault's suggestions further. Calvin Thomas, an American scholar concerned with the political applications of queer thinking for 'straight' men, has wondered whether 'desire must be taken literally', that is whether men interested in 'queering' their identities must perform certain acts (e.g. being anally penetrated, either by a man or by a woman with a strap-on) in order to justify their queer identification. In calling into question assumptions regarding at what level – bodily practice or political affiliation or fantasy – queer operates, Thomas retains the Foucaldian interest in challenging the notion that what we do is reducible to who we are, or that identity is literally readable in desires and acts.[25]

The ideas that parody and play are strategic political tools, and that identities can be *constituted* through practices and bodily acts, rather than *discovered* using the tools of psychoanalysis, have been key in the development of queer theory as a mode of political and academic praxis. However, certain scholars, such as Tim Dean, have argued convincingly that Lacan's strange, identity-disruptive texts must be dissociated from the conservative practice and politics of much clinical psychoanalysis, and may be profitably read alongside texts by thinkers such as Foucault. For Dean, Lacanian psychoanalysis 'is a queer theory in its own right'.[26] He stresses how, for Lacan, 'there is no privileged sexual activity or erotic narrative to which we should all aspire, no viable sexual norm for everybody, because desire's origins are multiple and its ambition no more specific than satisfaction'.[27] The aim of Dean's work is to conceptualise an impersonal account of desire by marrying Lacan's insistence that in the unconscious there is no gender, no 'proper' object of desire, with the Foucaldian ambition to 'shift beyond sexuality as the primary register in which we make sense of ourselves'.[28] Foucault and Lacan are presented in this convincing account as more compatible bedfellows than critical orthodoxy would allow us to think.

It is difficult, then, to summarise queer theory or reduce it to a number of assertions or precepts, and to say which methodologies and critical fields may or may not engage with it, as to do so is in many ways at odds with the spirit of queer. As we have seen, it is a non-totalising methodology which was born from, but is no longer identical with, gay and lesbian studies and gay history. Foucault was by no means the only inspiration for the development of this meta-theory. Derrida's deconstruction of binary thinking lent a key methodological tenet to queer, and Sedgwick's critique of knowledge/ignorance could not have been carried out without it. Despite this, Foucault's influence is nevertheless beyond question, and in some ways, queer is only now starting to respond to some of the challenges and questions set down by Foucault in the 1970s and early 1980s. The idea that a politics might be possible that would go beyond a narrow same-sex identitarian agenda and instead change the way in which we understand erotic relationality *altogether* beyond the categories of gay, straight, bi, SM etc. is already present in Foucault's musings in 1981:

> Rather than saying what we said at one time, 'Let's try to re-introduce homosexuality into the general norm of social relations,' let's say the reverse – 'No! Let's escape as much as possible from the type of relations that society proposes for us and try to create in the empty space where we are new relational possibilities.' By proposing a new relational *right*, we will see that nonhomosexual people can enrich their lives by changing their own schema of relations.
>
> (*EW i*, 160)

This is Foucault at his most utopian, proposing that the social body may be modified by the lessons to be learned from the practice of bodies and pleasures rather than that identities should be formed from the ways in which bodies and pleasures are understood (as sex and desire) in knowledge production. This is the articulation of both *the potential link* and the *current disparity* between the model of the disciplinary society and the model of the *askesis* of sexual selfhood: whereas in our present time the latter would be at odds with the former, in a queer space and time to come the former might somehow issue from the latter.

At the end of Didier Eribon's *Hérésies*, in a chapter dedicated to the right-wing French psychoanalytic response to the prospect of gay parenting (nothing less than the dissolution of the entire Symbolic order, according to certain extremist Millerians), the author evokes the same Foucaldian quotation as I have just considered; that is Foucault's call for 'new relational possibilities'.[29] Eribon cites 'le pacs' as the closest France has come to a social and legal institution that accepts partnerships between same-sex as well as heterosexual couples. ('Le pacs' is very similar to the institution of civil partnership recently introduced in the UK.) But this is very far, Eribon argues, from the alternative ways of conceiving relationality that Foucault was proposing – 'between two – or several persons' and encompassing 'multiple forms of bond (sexual, emotional, friendly)'.[30] Foucault's vision took its inspiration – heuristically – from ancient culture and from San Francisco bathhouses in the 1980s, organs of relationality that could not look more different from the secularised form of marriage currently offered to gay couples in some parts of Europe. While the liberal project of acquiring relational rights is an urgent anti-homophobic political project, the radical potential espied in Foucault's writings more than thirty years ago for undoing what scholars of polyamory today have dubbed 'mononormativity' must not be underestimated either.[31] Foucault's proto-queer imaginings of relational possibilities defined by plurality and diffuseness – by a constant negotiation between the processes of self-creation and the disciplinary inscription of new forms of sexual relationality in social and legal codes – go far beyond anything we have seen translated into contemporary policy making and thematise the most challenging tension visible throughout Foucault's work on self and relationality.

Afterword

In this book I have attempted to provide a guide to reading and understanding Foucault's major texts in their historical and philosophical contexts. This general aim has been inflected with a particular critical interest in the insights Foucault brings to the ways in which sexuality, subjectivity, and categories of abnormality (madness, criminality, sexual 'deviance') are constructed and made to function within political discourses for normalising purposes. At the same time, my focus on Foucault as a politicised thinker, a radical demystifier of commonplaces, has been combined with a regard for his own fascination with the extreme, the unusual and the eccentric. Without wanting to trace this 'fascination' to a biographical source or reduce it to a 'personality trait', I have sought instead to point to the paradoxical and rich instances within the stuff of Foucaldian textuality where critiques of the subject of experience shade into striking and jubilant descriptions of 'limit experiences' expressed in and accessed via literary language; where suspicion of the identity category of homosexuality overlaps with an enthusiastic and utopian vision of a post-heterosexual 'mono-sexual' politics; where aesthetics and ethics are made – despite their apparently incompatible fit – to co-exist in a project of 'self-stylisation'.

If readers continue to be interested in Foucault – and all the signs suggest that this is the case – it is, perhaps, because these very tensions and internal contradictions make him one of the most relevant thinkers for our current age. Foucault, as I have shown in this book, refers frequently in his archaeological and genealogical analyses to those figures who straddle two epistemic moments: Don Quixote, who pursues a quest according to rules of affinity that no longer operate in the historical episteme of Cervantes's book; the Marquis de Sade, inaugurator of the modern mode of writing, pushing representation to its limit until it self-destructs in a repetitive frenzy. Foucault himself, I would argue, may be just such a transitional figure. Although he died more than twenty years ago, the works he has left behind continue to have relevance – as I hope to have shown with reference to specific texts and concepts – for our political, cultural and philosophical lives today. Foucault's textual production may be said to mark the overlap of two intellectual epochs: the structuralist and

118

post-structuralist moment, which inaugurated a suspicious critique of human-istic principles (and to which Foucault contributed in his own lifetime), and a more recent and more radical offshoot (it would be out of keeping with a Fou-caldian genealogy to say 'continuation' or 'advance'), characterised variously as post-humanism, post-modernism and even (as I heard at a conference recently) post-post-modernism. That the subject of the cogito is an unstable fiction is, in critical theory circles, already old hat. But the centrality of our place in the world as 'human beings' is increasingly and materially being thrown into doubt by discursive reflections on the virtual reality of the internet and its capacity for extra-corporeal, plural and depersonalised communication; by the cyborg the-ory associated with Donna Haraway, which argues that, owing to our increased interaction with technology and reliance on machines, we are no longer wholly organic or human biological entities;[1] and by a strand of post-human eco-criticism that argues that the arrogance of human-centric thought has been responsible for the current ecological threat to which the planet is perceived to be subject. When writing in 1966 of 'man' as a temporary historical construct liable to be 'erased, like a face drawn in sand at the edge of the sea' (*OT*, p. 422), Foucault presciently announced the climate of our late twentieth and early twenty-first-century technocracy, and the concomitant prominence that issues such as the ones I have listed above would gain in both media and intellectual circles. TV and newspaper debates about global warming or the 'dangers' of the internet co-exist with apprehensions of ontology as post-humanist in the Ivory Tower. Scholars, politicians and citizens are divided on the meanings of the political, ecological and ideological conditions in which we live. For some cyborg feminists such as Haraway technology and virtual reality mark the end of the belief that biology is destiny and signal the disentanglement of women from social roles and behaviours defined by their corporeality. (Post-human may also be post-gender according to theorists such as Judith Halberstam.[2]) Others argue that new technologies and the renunciation of traditional modal-ities of communication mark a relational and intellectual decline and view the 'death' of a traditional view of the human subject pessimistically.

Since Foucault argued consistently, both in writings on medicine and on literature, that modern consciousness is increasingly predicated on a perception of death, of finitude, and indeed predicted the death of 'man' *qua* category, it is no wonder that his contemporaries and the reading public wondered what to make of him, and asked questions about the status of his pronouncements that are similar to those questions posed by our own contemporaries with regard to the discourses that surround us today. Were his statements serious harbingers of doom or clever and refreshing practical jokes at the expense of humanistic and Enlightenment thought? Was he 'an irrationalist, a nihilist' (*TS*, p. 13) as some thought, or a prankster, as Deleuze resolutely claimed?[3] While none of these terms appears wholly accurate, I have suggested here that Foucault's play with language and knowledge means that the spirit of his work is closer to Deleuze's perspective than to the one that suggests a thoroughgoing nihilism. Transcending all these labels, however, and irreducible to any of them, Foucault remains one of the most innovative, exciting and, I have been arguing, *relevant* thinkers of the twentieth century.

Notes

1. Life, texts, contexts

1. Didier Eribon, *Michel Foucault* [1989], trans. Betsy Wing (Cambridge, Mass: Harvard University Press, 1991), p. ix.
2. Ibid.
3. Those requiring an accessible study of Michel Foucault's thought in the context of his life may consult David Macey's helpful *Michel Foucault*, Critical Lives (London: Reaktion Books, 2004). Other notable biographies are Eribon's *Michel Foucault*, cited above; David Macey, *The Lives of Michel Foucault* (London: Hutchinson, 1993); and James Miller, *The Passion of Michel Foucault* (London: Harper Collins, 1993). On some of the dangers of biographical criticism, however, see Gary Gutting's critique of Miller's book, which, he claims, relies heavily on making causal links between Foucault's own penchant for extreme or 'limit' experiences and the extremity found in his writings and arguments. Gutting argues that Miller is guilty of reducing the complexity of Foucault's work to the singularity of the biographer's own particular critical slant on the thinker's personality (Gary Gutting, 'Michel Foucault: A User's Guide', *The Cambridge Companion to Foucault*, ed. Gary Gutting, Cambridge University Press, 1994, p. 23).
4. Friedrich Nietzsche, *The Gay Science*, trans. Walter Kaufmann (New York: Vintage, 1974), p. 232.
5. Foucault offered as an example of the specific intellectual Dr Edith Rose, who was sacked from her post of prison psychiatrist at Toul when she denounced to the press the common mistreatment of prisoners and the pressure under which she had been placed to withhold medical treatment from them. (For more, see Macey, *Foucault*, pp. 98–9.)
6. Critics and biographers provide strikingly divergent accounts of the length of time that Foucault was actually a member of the Party. Accurate records are hard to track down and incomplete. Foucault himself admitted to being a member for 'a few months or a bit longer', *DE i*, p. 666 (untranslated; my translation).
7. Cited in Otto Friedrich, 'France's Philosopher of Power', *Time* (16 November 1981), pp. 147–8.
8. Cited in article on 'Georges Dumézil' in *Encyclopedia of Modern French Thought*, ed. Christopher John Murray (New York: Taylor and Francis, 2004), pp. 189–91.

9. 'Life, Experience and Science', in *EW ii*, pp. 465–78.
10. I have modified the translation of this passage, as Alan Sheridan's original is misleading. Where I translated 'experience' it gives 'to what I called an "experiment"'. This is a case of a translator trying too hard to avoid a common 'false friend' in French. (*Expérience* should often, but not in this case, be translated 'experiment'.)
11. See Macey, *Michel Foucault*, p. 73.
12. Cited ibid., p. 217.
13. See ibid., pp. 123–4. Macey explains: 'The title is a clever pun: its literal meaning is "gay foot" but *prendre son pied* is a slang expression meaning to have sexual pleasure or "to have an orgasm"' (p. 123).
14. See the interview 'Structuralism and Post-structuralism', *EW ii*, pp. 437–439.
15. Allan Megill, 'Foucault, Structuralism and the Ends of History', *The Journal of Modern History*, 51:3 (1979), 451–503.
16. Alan Sheridan, *Michel Foucault: The Will to Truth* (London: Tavistock, 1980).
17. Charles Lemert and Garth Gillan, *Michel Foucault: Social Theory and Transgression* (New York: Columbia University Press, 1982).
18. Dave Robinson, *Nietzsche and Postmodernism*, Postmodern Encounters (Reading: Totem Books, 1999), p. 44.
19. Friedrich Nietzsche, 'On Truth and Falsity in their Extra-Moral Sense' (1873), in *The Viking Portable Nietzsche*, trans. Walter Kaufmann (New York: The Viking Press, 1954), p. 42.
20. Ibid.
21. See, for the most accessible account of this critique, Gary Gutting, *Foucault: A Very Short Introduction* (Oxford University Press, 2005), pp. 43–53.
22. Nietzsche, *The Anti-Christ* [1888], in *The Viking Portable Nietzsche*, p. 656.
23. 'Structuralism and Post-Structuralism', *EW ii*, p. 447.
24. Gilles Deleuze, *Michel Foucault* [1986], trans. and ed. Seán Hand (New York and London: Continuum, 2006), p. 21.
25. E.g. *EW ii*, p. 419. (*DE ii*, p. 268).
26. Ibid.
27. Jean Piaget, *Structuralism*, cited in Megill, 'Foucault, Structuralism and the Ends of History', p. 470. Piaget, himself a committed structuralist who brought a scientific rigour to the endeavour, did not intend this description of Foucault's work to be flattering or positive, but Foucault, determined to reject the label of structuralist, may well have appreciated it never the less.
28. Clare O'Farrell, *Foucault: Historian or Philosopher* (Basingstoke: Macmillan, 1989).
29. Todd May, *Between Genealogy and Epistemology* (Pennsylvania: Penn State University Press, 1993).
30. Alan Petersen and Robin Bunton, eds., *Foucault, Health and Medicine* (London and New York: Routledge, 1997).

31. For more on the *Annales* school, see Peter Burke, *The French Histori- cal Revolution: The Annales School 1929–89* (Palo Alto: Stanford University Press, 1991) and François Dosse, *New History in France: The Triumph of the Annales,* trans. Peter V. Conroy Jr. (Urbana: University of Illinois Press, 1994).
32. 'Governmentality' in *The Foucault Effect: Studies in Governmentality,* ed. Graham Burchell, Colin Gordon and Peter Miller (London: Harvester Wheatsheaf, 1991).
33. Ibid., p. 91.
34. Ibid., p. 95.
35. Lois McNay, *Foucault: A Critical Introduction* (Oxford: Polity, 1994), p. 134.
36. Ann Laura Stoler, *Race and the Education of Desire: Foucault's History of Sex- uality and the Colonial Order of Things* (Durham, NC: Duke University Press, 1995).

2. Works: madness and medicine

1. See Macey, *Michel Foucault,* pp. 29–30.
2. Ibid., pp. 20–1.
3. In this chapter, I shall refer to both works, citing from *The History of Madness* (*HM*) any vital passages omitted in the earlier and shorter English translation (*MC*). I shall refer generally to *Histoire de la folie* as *The History of Madness* or *History* throughout, where my remarks pertain to the French original rather than a specific English edition.
4. When referring to 'classical' to mean 'early modern', I shall use a lower case 'c'. 'Classical' with an upper case 'C' will denote ancient history and culture.
5. Gary Gutting, *Michel Foucault's Archaeology of Scientific Reason* (Cambridge Uni- versity Press, 1989).
6. Rosi Braidotti, *Patterns of Dissonance: A Study of Women in Contemporary Philosophy* (Cambridge: Polity Press, 1991), p. 56.
7. For an account of the relationship between Foucault's work and the anti-medicine movement, see Thomas Osborne, 'On Anti-Medicine and Clinical Reason', in Colin Jones and Roy Porter (eds.), *Reassessing Foucault: Power, Medicine and the Body* (London and New York: Routledge, 1994), pp. 28–47.
8. H. C. Erik Midelfort, 'Madness and Civilization in Early Modern Europe: A Reap- praisal of Michel Foucault', in *After the Reformation: Essays in Honor of J. H. Hexter,* ed. B. C. Malament (Philadelphia: University of Pennsylvania Press, 1980), pp. 247– 65.
9. For a commentary on Foucault's tendency to ignore non-Western institutions and practices, and his partial and inadequate treatment of ethnicity and race, see Sander L. Gilman, *Difference and Pathology: Stereotypes of Sexuality, Race and Madness* (Ithaca: Cornell University Press, 1985).

10. Jürgen Habermas, *The Philosophical Discourse of Modernity* (Cambridge: Polity, 1987), p. 291; Gillian Rose, *Dialectic of Nihilism: Poststructuralism and Law* (Oxford: Blackwell, 1984), pp. 171–207.
11. McNay, *Foucault: A Critical Introduction*, p. 26.
12. Andrew Scull, 'Michel Foucault's *History of Madness*', *History of the Human Sciences*, 3:1 (1990), 57–67.
13. Jacques Derrida, 'Cogito et histoire de la folie', in *L'Ecriture et la différence* (Paris: Seuil, 1967), pp. 51–99; 'Cogito and the History of Madness', in *Writing and Difference*, trans. Alan Bass (London: Routledge and Kegan Paul, 1978), pp. 31–63.
14. Derrida, 'Cogito and the History of Madness', p. 36.
15. Laurent Muchielli, ed., *Histoire de la criminologie française* (Paris: L'Harmattan, 1996).
16. See David Armstrong, 'Bodies of Knowledge/Knowledge of Bodies' in Jones and Porter, *Reassessing Foucault*, pp. 17–27. The sociological studies he cites are by Waddington and Jewson.

3. Works: the death of man

1. Megill, 'Foucault, Structuralism and the Ends of History', p. 475.
2. Jean-Paul Sartre, 'Jean-Paul Sartre répond', *L'Arc* (30 October 1966), 87–96.
3. 'In *Madness and Civilization* and *The Birth of the Clinic* I wanted precisely to define the different relationships between these different domains. I took, for example, the epistemological domain of medicine and that of the institutions of repression . . . but I perceived that things were more complicated than I had believed in the first two works, that the discursive domains didn't always obey the structures that had common practical domains and associated institutions, that they obeyed on the other hand structures common to other epistemological domains' (*FL*, pp. 18–19).
4. Peter L. Berger and Thomas Luckman, *The Social Construction of Reality* [1966] (Harmondsworth: Penguin, 1971), p. 27.
5. Ibid., p. 207.
6. George Huppert, 'Divinatio et Eruditio: Thoughts on Foucault', *History and Theory*, 13, 1974, 191–207.
7. G. S. Rousseau, 'Whose Enlightenment? Not Man's: the Case of Michel Foucault', *Eighteenth-Century Studies*, 6, 1972–3, 238–56.
8. Lemert and Gillan, *Michel Foucault: Social Theory and Transgression*, p. 131.
9. Deleuze, *Foucault*, p. 3.
10. See Lemert and Gillan, *Michel Foucault: Social Theory and Transgression*, p. 51.
11. Ibid., p. 135.
12. Hubert Dreyfus and Paul Rabinow, *Michel Foucault: Beyond Structuralism and Hermeneutics* (Brighton: Harvester Press, 1982).

13. See Ernesto Laclau and Chantal Mouffe, *Hegemony and Socialist Strategy: Towards a Radical Democratic Politics* (London: Verso, 1985).
14. Macey, *Michel Foucault*, p. 72.

4. Works: authors and texts

1. Terry Eagleton, *Literary Theory: An Introduction* (London and New York: Routledge, 1983).
2. Ann Jefferson and David Robey, *Modern Literary Theory: A Comparative Introduction* (London: Batsford, 1982).
3. The most extreme example of Roland Barthes in his high-structural phase is probably the article 'Introduction to the Structural Analysis of Narratives' (1966), in which he argues that narrative significance depends not on its mimetic function or content, but on the inner logic that texts create by their opening and closing semantic sequences. In *A Barthes Reader*, ed. Susan Sontag (New York: Hill and Wang, 1983), pp. 251–95.
4. Roman Jakobson and Claude Lévi-Strauss, 'Charles Baudelaire's "Les Chats"' (1962), in Roman Jakobson, *Language in Literature*, ed. Krystyna Pomorska and Stephen Rudy (Cambridge, Mass.: Harvard University Press, 1988), pp. 180–97.
5. Georges Bataille, *Eroticism*, trans. Mary Dalwood (London: Marion Boyars, 1962), p. 11.
6. Georges Bataille, *The Accursed Share*, trans. Robert Hurley, 3 vols. (New York: Zone, 1988–91), vol ii, p. 84.
7. Bataille, *Eroticism*, p. 63.
8. One of the few attempts to compare Foucaldian and Lévinasian ethics, and to read them in dialogue with each other, can be found in Barry Smart, 'Foucault, Lévinas and the Subject of Responsibility', in *The Later Foucault: Politics and Philosophy*, ed. Jeremy Moss (London: Sage, 1998), pp. 78–92. However, Smart focuses on Foucault's late ethics of the 'care for the self' and compares this unfavourably with Lévinas's focus on an ethics of alterity. A reading that takes into account Foucault's broader corpus may produce unacknowledged latent affinities, despite the obvious differences of the two thinkers' ethical (and spiritual) agendas.
9. Nietzsche, *The Gay Science*, p. xxiv.
10. Simon During, *Foucault and Literature: Towards a Genealogy of Writing* (London and New York: Routledge, 1992), p. 85.
11. Deleuze, *Foucault*, p. 8.
12. Cited in During, *Foucault and Literature*, p. 68.
13. Ibid., p. 76.
14. Gilles Deleuze and Félix Guattari, *Anti-Oedipus: Capitalism and Schizophrenia* [1972], trans. Robert Hurley *et al.* (London: Athlone Press, 1984).
15. See especially Miller, *The Passion of Michel Foucault*.

5. Works: crime and punishment

1. For critiques of the gender politics of Foucault's interpretation of *I Pierre Rivière*, see Jill Forbes, 'Matricides', *L'Esprit Créateur* 42 (spring, 2002), 62–70 and Josephine McDonagh, 'Do or Die: Problems of Agency and Gender in the Aesthetics of Murder', *Genders* 5 (summer, 1989), 120–34.
2. See McDonagh, 'Do or Die'.
3. A notable exception to my assertion that Foucault's language is seldom studied is Dan Beer's *Michael Foucault: Form and Power* (Oxford: Legenda, University of Oxford, 2002), although this work concentrates only on a close reading of the first volume of the *History of Sexuality*.
4. Anthony Giddens, *The Constitution of Society: Outline of the Theory of Structuration* (Cambridge: Polity Press, 1984).
5. Erving Goffman, *Asylums* (Harmondsworth: Penguin, 1961).
6. Peter Dews, *Logics of Disintegration: Post-Structuralist Thought and the Claims of Critical Theory* (London: Verso, 1987).

6. Works: *The History of Sexuality*

1. See Arnold I. Davidson, 'Ethics as Ascetics: Foucault, the History of Ethics and Ancient Thought', in Gutting (ed.), *The Cambridge Companion to Foucault*, p. 117.
2. For more introductory information on the history of sexology, see especially Joseph Bristow, *Sexuality* (London and New York: Routledge), pp. 12–61, and Gert Hekma, 'A History of Sexology: Social and Historical Aspects of Sexuality', in *From Sappho to de Sade: Moments in the History of Sexuality*, ed. Jan Bremmer (London and New York: Routledge, 1991), pp. 173–93.
3. I have modified the translation here. Hurley coins the unhelpful neologism 'naturality' which I have altered to the more comprehensible 'natural status'.
4. Peter Cryle has pointed out that Diderot's text is not the most appropriate illustration Foucault could have chosen of the scientific exhortation to confess sexual deeds in literary form, since it belongs to the eighteenth-century tradition of *libertinage* rather than the nineteenth-century genre of medical literature. In *libertinage* speaking about sex was a matter of pleasure, but no 'truth' about a 'subject of sex' was adduced from confession. Peter Cryle, 'On the Unsteadiness of Sexual Truth in Eighteenth-Century France', unpublished paper, 2007.
5. I particularly like Lemert and Gillan's translation and explanation of the concept: 'Affective mechanisms of sexuality (*dispositifs de sexualité*): though translated, in the standard American edition, as "deployment of sexuality", this phrase should indicate a general social mechanism whereby the knowledge and practice of sexuality is dispersed through society': Lemert and Gillan, *Michel Foucault: Social Theory and Transgression*, p. 127.

6. For an intelligent and comprehensive account of the different European strands of Degeneration theory, see Daniel Pick, *Faces of Degeneration: A European Disorder, c. 1848–c. 1918* (Cambridge University Press, 1989).
7. Luc Ferry and Alain Renault, *French Philosophy of the Sixties: An Essay on Anti-humanism*, trans. M. Cattani (Amherst: University of Massachusetts Press, 1990), 107–21.
8. Lois McNay, *Foucault and Feminism: Power, Gender and the Self* (Cambridge: Polity, 1992), p. 48.
9. John Rajchman, *Truth and Eros: Foucault, Lacan and the Question of Ethics* (London and New York: Routledge, 1991).
10. Ibid., p. 1.

7. Critical reception

1. See Jana Sawicki, *Disciplining Foucault: Feminism, Power and the Body* (New York and London: Routledge, 1991), p. 1.
2. Sandra Lee Bartky, 'Foucault, Femininity, and the Modernization of Patriarchal Power', in Irene Diamond and Lee Quinby, eds., *Feminism and Foucault: Reflections on Resistance* (Boston: Northeastern University Press, 1988), pp. 61–86. Other significant feminist critiques of Foucault include Rosi Braidotti, *Patterns of Dissonance* and Patricia O'Brien, 'Crime and Punishment as Historical Problem', *Journal of Social History*, 11 (1978), 508–20.
3. Sawiki, *Disciplining Foucault*, p. 11.
4. Diamond and Quinby, 'Introduction', *Feminism and Foucault*, pp. ix–x.
5. Ibid., p. xii.
6. John Rajchman, 'Ethics After Foucault', *Social Text*, 13/14 (winter/spring 1986), 166–7.
7. Jean Grimshaw, 'Practices of Freedom', in *Up Against Foucault: Explorations of Some Tensions Between Foucault and Feminism*, ed. Caroline Ramazanoglu (London and New York: Routledge, 1993), 51–72.
8. Ibid., pp. 66–7.
9. McNay, *Foucault and Feminism*, p. 4.
10. Ibid., p. 6.
11. Adrienne Rich, 'Compulsory Heterosexuality and Lesbian Existence', in *Signs: Journal of Women in Culture and Society*, 5 (1980), 631–60.
12. Ladelle McWhorter, *Bodies and Pleasures: Foucault and the Politics of Sexual Normalization* (Bloomington and Indianapolis: Indiana University Press, 1999), p. 1.
13. Ibid., pp. 3–4.
14. Mary McIntosh, 'The Homosexual Role' [1968], in *The Making of the Modern Homosexual*, ed. Kenneth Plummer (London: Hutchinson), 1981, pp. 30–44.
15. French sociologist Marie-Hélène Bourcier has recently pointed out in an untranslated work that while doubtless providing a key part of the framework for Butler's

conceptualisation of performative gender, Foucault himself was not explicitly interested in the figure of the 'gender bender', in the politics of drag, or in exploiting the 'distinction between biological sex and gender' (*Queer Zones: Politique des identités sexuelles et des savoirs* [2001], Paris: Editions Amsterdam, 2006, p. 81, my translation). This is a continuation of the Anglo-American critique of Foucault as having a masculinist or androcentric blind spot.

16. Eve Kosofsky Sedgwick, *Epistemology of the Closet*, Berkeley and Los Angeles: University of California Press, 1990, p. 1.

17. Ibid., p. 4.

18. Ibid., p. 4.

19. Foucault's statement that 'we must not exclude identity if people find their pleasure through it' rings with a certain irony twenty years into the development of queer. Since one of the key strategies of queer is to problematise fixity and identity, being fixated – liking only one type of pleasure or relation – has become as stigmatised by queer theorists as it is by sexologists and psychoanalysts, for whom a perversion is only a perversion if it is singular and fixated. On the tyranny of plurality, see Brad Epps, 'The Fetish of Fluidity', in *Homosexuality and Psychoanalysis*, ed. Tim Dean and Christopher Lane, pp. 412–31.

20. Alexander Doty, 'Queer Theory' in *The Oxford Guide to Film Studies*, ed. John Hill and Pamela Church Gibson (Oxford University Press, 1998), p. 149. The italics are mine.

21. Judith Butler, 'Imitation and Gender Insubordination' [1991], in *The Lesbian and Gay Studies Reader*, ed. Henry Abelove, Michèle Aina Barale and David M. Halperin (London: Routledge, 1993), pp. 307–20.

22. Stephen Engel, 'Making a Minority', in *Handbook of Lesbian and Gay Studies*, ed. Diane Richardson and Steven Seidman (London: Sage, 2002), pp. 377–402.

23. David Halperin, *Saint Foucault: Towards a Gay Hagiography* (Oxford University Press, 1995), p. 4.

24. Tamsin Spargo, *Foucault and Queer Theory*, Postmodern Encounters (Cambridge: Icon Books, 1999), pp. 33–4.

25. See: Calvin Thomas, 'Must Desire Be Taken Literally?', *Parallax*, 8:4 (2002), 46–56, and Thomas (ed.), *Straight with a Twist: Queer Theory and the Subject of Heterosexuality* (Urbana and Chicago: University of Illinois Press, 2000).

26. Tim Dean, *Beyond Sexuality* (Chicago University Press, 2000), p. 265.

27. Ibid., p. 196.

28. Ibid., p. 88.

29. Didier Eribon, *Hérésies: essais sur la théorie de la sexualité* (Paris: Fayard, 2003), p. 276. My translation.

30. Ibid., p. 277. My translation.

31. Scholars and activists of polyamory (consensual, honest non-monogamy) argue that the social privileging and legal recognition of coupledom (mononormativity) constitutes a normalising and excluding discourse. See the bible of polyamory: Dossie Easton and Catherine A. Liszt, *The Ethical Slut: A Guide to Infinite Sexual*

Possibilities (California: Greenery Press, 1997). See also Meg Barker, 'This is my partner, and this is my partner's partner: Constructing a polyamorous identity in a monogamous world', *Journal of Constructivist Psychology*, 18 (2004), 75–88, and Marcia Munson and Judith P. Stelboum, eds., *The Lesbian Polyamory Reader* (New York: Harrington Park Press, 1999).

Afterword

1. Donna Haraway, 'A Cyborg Manifesto: Science, Technology, and Socialist-Feminism in the Late Twentieth Century' in *Simians, Cyborgs and Women: The Reinvention of Nature* (London and New York: Routledge, 1991), pp. 149–81.
2. Halberstam explains what she means by this term in her essay on *The Silence of The Lambs*, 'Skinflick: Posthuman Gender in Jonathan Demme's *The Silence of the Lambs*', *Camera Obscura*, 27 (Sept. 1991), 37–52.
3. Deleuze, *Foucault*, p. 21.

Selected further reading

Barker, Philip. *Michel Foucault: Subversions of the Subject*. London and New York: Harvester Wheatsheaf, 1993. [A study of the centrality of the complex concept of the subject in Foucault's work.]

Beer, Dan. *Foucault: Form and Power*. Oxford: Legenda, European Humanities Research Centre, University of Oxford, 2002. [A sensitive reading of Foucault's use of language in *The Will to Knowledge*.]

Bernauer, James. *Michel Foucault's Force of Flight: Towards an Ethics for Thought*. New Jersey and London: Humanities Press International, 1990. [A reflection on Foucault's philosophical corpus as a work of ethics.]

Bernauer, James and David Rasmussen, eds. *The Final Foucault*. Cambridge, Mass: MIT Press, 1987–8. [A selection of scholarly essays about Foucault's late work and some interviews with Foucault from his final years.]

Bristow, Joseph. 'Chapter 4: Discursive Desires', in *Sexuality*. London and New York: Routledge, 1997. [A good introduction to the place of Foucault's work in modern critical approaches to sexuality.]

Clifford, Michael. *Political Genealogy after Foucault: Savage Identities*. London and New York: Routledge, 2001. [An account of a radical politics of freedom via a reading of Foucault's cultural and political critique.]

Davidson, Arnold I., ed. *Foucault and his Interlocutors*. University of Chicago Press, 1997. [A good contextualisation of Foucault's works in the light of his contemporary intellectual climate.]

Diamond, Irene and Lee Quinby, eds. *Feminism and Foucault: Reflections on Resistance*. Boston: Northeastern University Press, 1988. [A collection of essays on the possible value of Foucault's work for feminist criticism and practice.]

Dumm, Thomas. *Michel Foucault and the Politics of Freedom*. London: Sage, 1994. [Reads Foucault's work alongside contemporary liberal discourse to challenge commonplace understandings of what might be meant by 'political freedom'.]

During, Simon. *Foucault and Literature: Towards a Genealogy of Writing*. London and New York: Routledge, 1992. [A full-length account of the importance of literature in the whole of Foucault's corpus.]

Eribon, Didier. *Michel Foucault* [1989], trans. Betsy Wing, Cambridge, Mass:
    Harvard University Press, 1991. [Biography of Foucault by France's
    foremost contemporary gay theorist.]

Goldstein, Jan, ed. *Foucault and the Writing of History*. Oxford: Blackwell, 1994.
    [An account of Foucault's historiographical methods.]

Gutting, Gary. *Michel Foucault's Archaeology of Scientific Reason*. Cambridge
    University Press, 1989. [A detailed and contextualising study of
    Foucault's 'archaeological' works.]

Gutting, Gary, ed. *The Cambridge Companion to Foucault*. Cambridge University
    Press, 1994. [A collection of essays by leading Foucault scholars on many
    major aspects of his work.]

Halperin, David. *Saint Foucault: Towards a Gay Hagiography*. Oxford University
    Press, 1995. [An account of Foucault's importance for the gay and
    lesbian movement (especially in America) and for queer theory.]

Han, Béatrice. *Foucault's Critical Project: Between the Transcendental and the
    Historical*. Stanford University Press, 2005. [A careful exploration of the
    intersection of philosophy and history in Foucault's works.]

Jones, Colin and Roy Porter, eds. *Reassessing Foucault: Power, Medicine and the
    Body*. London and New York: Routledge, 1994. [A series of essays from
    different disciplinary perspectives exploring the importance of
    Foucault's work for debates about the history of medicine and
    institutions.]

Lemert, Charles and Garth Gillan. *Michel Foucault: Social Theory and
    Transgression*. New York: Columbia University Press, 1982. [A study of
    the political radicalism of Foucault's critique of social organisation.]

McLaren, Margaret. *Feminism, Foucault and Embodied Subjectivity*. Albany:
    SUNY Press, 2002. [A feminist reflection on Foucault's theory of power
    and embodiment.]

McNay, Lois. *Foucault and Feminism: Power, Gender and the Self*. Cambridge:
    Polity, 1992. [A study of Foucault's work through the lens of feminism.]
    Foucault: A Critical Introduction. Oxford: Polity, 1994. [An introduction to
    Foucault's works aimed mainly at students of political science.]

McWhorter, Ladelle. *Bodies and Pleasures: Foucault and the Politics of Sexual
    Normalization*. Bloomington and Indianapolis: Indiana University Press,
    1999. [A semi-autobiographical account of the relevance of Foucault's
    work for the experience of lived lesbian identity.]

Macey, David. *The Lives of Michel Foucault*. London: Hutchinson, 1993. [A
    sensitive and nuanced biography of Foucault.]
    Foucault Critical Lives, London: Reaktion Books, 2004. [An introduction to
    Foucault's work through his life and intellectual/political contexts.]

Mahon, Michael. *Foucault's Nietzschean Genealogy: Truth, Power and the Subject*.
    Albany: SUNY Press, 1992. [A study of the importance of Nietzsche for
    Foucault's genealogical writings.]

May, Todd. *The Philosophy of Foucault*. Chesham: Acumen, 2006. [An attempt to
    identify philosophical questions that run through the whole of

Foucault's corpus, transcending the common division of his work into three stages (archaeology, genealogy, ethics).]

Megill, Allan. 'Foucault, Structuralism and the Ends of History', *The Journal of Modern History*, 51.3, 1979, 451–503. [An essay situating Foucault's work between historiography and structuralism.]

Prophets of Extremity: Nietzsche, Heidegger, Foucault, Derrida. Berkeley: University of California Press, 1985. [A book which reads four thinkers, including Foucault, as philosophers of extremity operating in a broad genealogy, but with notable differences of agenda.]

Miller, James. *The Passion of Michel Foucault.* London: Harper Collins, 1993. [A biography of Foucault which attributes the content and themes of his work to his personal tastes and lived experiences.]

Moss, Jeremy, ed. *The Later Foucault: Politics and Philosophy.* London: Sage, 1998. [A reflection on Foucault's late work on ethics for politics and philosophy.]

Rajchman, John. *Michel Foucault: The Freedom of Philosophy.* New York: Columbia University Press, 1985. [A book which situates Foucault as a historian of systems of thought rather than a positivistic philosopher.]

'Ethics after Foucault', *Social Text*, 13/14 (winter/spring, 1996), 165–83. [An account of the importance of Foucault's ethical writing for subsequent thought.]

Ramazanoglu, Caroline, ed. *Up Against Foucault: Exploration of Some Tensions Between Foucault and Feminism.* London and New York: Routledge, 1993. [A series of scholarly essays exploring the difficult and fruitful relationship between Foucault and feminism.]

Sawicki, Jana. *Disciplining Foucault: Feminism, Power and the Body.* London and New York: Routledge, 1991. [An argument for the usefulness of Foucault's work for a non-essentialist feminism.]

Scott, Charles. *The Question of Ethics: Nietzsche, Foucault, Heidegger.* Bloomington: Indiana University Press, 1990. [An exploration of Foucault's version of ethics, alongside Nietzsche's and Heidegger's.]

Sheridan, Alan. *Michel Foucault: The Will to Truth.* London: Tavistock, 1980. [A study of Foucault's corpus with emphasis on his role as a political thinker.]

Simons, Jon. *Foucault and the Political.* London and New York: Routledge, 1995. [A systematic review of Foucault's political theory.]

Smart, Barry. *Michel Foucault: Marxism and Critique.* London: Tavistock, 1985. [A book-length exploration of Foucault's ambivalent relationship with Marxist thought.]

Smart, Barry, ed. *Foucault: Critical Assessments.* London and New York: Routledge, 1994–5. [A general introduction to the works of Foucault.]

Spargo, Tamsin. *Foucault and Queer Theory*. Postmodern Encounters, Cambridge: Icon Books, 1999. [A short introduction to queer theory accounting for Foucault's place within the development of the theory.]

Stoler, Ann Laura. *Race and the Education of Desire: Foucault's History of Sexuality and the Colonial Order of Things*. Durham, N.C.: Duke University Press, 1995. [A look at some potential uses of Foucault's analysis of power and sexuality for the theorisation of colonialism.]

Index

The Cambridge Introductions to . . .

Lightning Source UK Ltd.
Milton Keynes UK
UKOW032230221112

202564UK00002B/56/P